THE DHARMA FLOWER SUTRA

The WONDERFUL DHARMA LOTUS FLOWER SUTRA.

Translated into English by
Tripitaka Master Kumarajiva of Yao Ch'in

Volume 7,

Chapter 7 : The Analogy of the Transformed City

with the commentary of
TRIPITAKA MASTER HUA

Translated into English by
The Buddhist Text Translation Society
San Francisco
1980

6/1981
Rel.

Translated by the Buddhist Text Translation Society

Primary translation: Bhikshuni Heng-yin
Reviewed by: Bhikshuni Heng-ch'ih
Edited by: Upasika Kuo-lin Lethcoe

Certified by: The Venerable Master Hua

Printed in the United States of America

First printing--1980

For information address:
      Sino American Buddhist Association
      Dharma Realm Buddhist University
      Gold Mountain Monastery
      1731 15th Street
      San Francisco, California 94103
      U.S.A.
      (415) 621-5202
      (415) 861-9672

ISBN   0-917512-67-7

Acknowledgements:

Cover: Bhikshuni Heng-chieh
Index: Bhikshuni Heng-ming
English calligraphy (Sutra text and other) Jerri-jo
Illuminated letters: Kuo-ling Pecaites
Graphics and layout: Jerri-jo Idarius and
   Kuo-ling Pecaites
Photo of the Master: Kuo-ying Brevoort
Commentary typed by: Upasika Kuo-shan

Table of Contents

Buddhist Text Translation Society
Eight Regulations

A translator must free himself or herself from the motives of personal fame and reputation.

A translator must cultivate an attitude free from arrogance and conceit.

A translator must refrain from aggrandizing himself or herself and denigrating others.

A translator must not establish himself or herself as the standard of correctness and suppress the work of others with his or her faultfinding.

A translator must take the Buddha-mind as his or her own mind.

A translator must use the wisdom of the Selective Dharma Eye to determine true principles.

A translator must request the Elder Virtuous Ones of the ten directions to certify his or her translations.

A translator must endeavor to propagate the teachings by printing sutras, shastra texts, and vinaya texts when the translations are certified as being correct.

TRIPITAKA
MASTER HUA

OUTLINE: CHAPTER SEVEN

Chapter 7: The Analogy of the Transformed City

This is the seventh of the twenty-eight chapters of The Dharma Flower Sutra. What is meant by "Transformed"? It means to create something out of nothing, and to turn something back into nothing. Most people don't understand this doctrine. It is inconceivable and cannot be understood with the mind or expressed in words. "City" is a large town. People build cities to protect themselves from invaders.

Where does the transformation come from? It comes from the Buddha's spiritual penetrations. That is how, out of nothing, something can appear. Originally, the City did not exist, but now it appears. Once it appears, it is given the name "Transformed City."

The first thing we should understand about the Transformed City is that there is no such thing! It is an unreal city, created through transformation. It is an unreal city, an expedient city, an expedient Dharma, as it were. It is an expedient Dharma used to cross over expedient people. It is all entirely unreal: the city, the people, and the Dharma are all unreal.

"What's the use of it all, if it's all unreal?" you ask.

If you don't understand what is unreal, you will be unable to find the true. The Transformed City is a place where the Treasure Trove is kept. The Transformed City is the Provisional, while the Treasure Trove is the Real. Basically, the Transformed City doesn't exist at all. If it were real, it wouldn't be called a "Transformed City"; it would just be called a city. The analogy contains those of the Two Vehicles: the Sound Hearer Vehicle and the Conditioned Enlightened Vehicle. Are there really Two Vehicles? No. There are not Two Vehicles. Then why do you talk about Two Vehicles? Because they don't exist! If they did exist, we wouldn't have to speak about them!

The Two Vehicles are expedient Dharma. So the Transformed City is an analogy for the Nirvana of the Two Vehicles. Nirvana means "not produced and not destroyed." Without production, there is no extinction; without extinction, there is no production. The Nirvana of the Two Vehicles is that taught by the Provisional Wisdom; it is an expedient. The Buddha used his expedient and provisional wisdom to set forth the Dharma of the Two Vehicles. Why did he do this? When you go to school, why do you start out in elementary school? Why don't you just start out going to the University? You could have your Ph.D. by the time you were ten. Wouldn't that be great? Skip elementary school and high school. Unfortunately, you can't do this. You have to start with elementary school. The Two Vehicles are like elementary school. The Bodhisattva Vehicle is like high school. The Buddha Vehicle is like the university.

So, when I was in Hong Kong, I said, "I don't teach elementary school. I teach only at the university level." In grade school you have to keep the kids interested by telling them stories, and so forth, for them to make any progress. You can teach some doctrine in High School, but it's not until they reach college that they can really learn something.

The Buddhadharma works in the same way. Originally, there weren't Two Vehicles. The Buddha set them up; just like, originally, we didn't need elementary school, except that kids are too young to understand what they need to know, and so an elementary school is set up to take care of them.

Now, the university gives out various degrees: the Bachelor's, the Master's and the Ph.D. There are a lot of distinctions there. And so, those of the Two Vehicles are like the elementary school. If you want to become a Buddha, you must start out in "elementary school," then go to "high school," and then to the "university." "High school" is like the Bodhisattva Path, and the "university" is like Buddhahood.

You will understand this analogy, because you have all been to school.

"Oh?" you think, "the Two Vehicles are just elementary school."

Don't get too attached to the idea. It's only an analogy, you know.

In Buddhism, the most important thing is to become a Buddha. But most people, if you told them right off that they should cultivate and become a Buddha, would be scared stiff. "What's that? Why should I become a Buddha? Arghh!!" Since they don't understand, you set up an "elementary school." Obviously, you can't give a small child a Ph.D., because he wouldn't even have the sense to know what it was, and he wouldn't value it at all. So, the Transformed City represents the Nirvana of the Two Vehicles, a provisionally spoken expedient term. Basically, there is no such thing, but because of the power of the provisionally spoken expedient, something appears out of nothing.

Someone hears this and starts to retreat, thinking, "Oh, so the Buddha lies. There's nothing there, and he says there's something there!"

There was nothing there, and then something was transformed. This is not a lie. It's a provisional expedient. He uses the substance of the teaching to teach and transform living beings. Living beings are taught to guard against delusive thoughts. They are taught to cut off the delusions of desire and views. This is called the Nirvana which leans towards emptiness. It leans one way; it is not the Middle Way.

There are four ways of explaining the Sutras: 1) according to causes and conditions, 2) according to the essentials of the teaching, 3) according to the roots, and 4) according to contemplation of the mind.

Here I shall use the first two to explain the concept of the Transformed City.

a) According to causes and conditions: The doctrine of one-sided emptiness causes living beings to "rest, to be led, and to enter." To "rest" refers to the teaching of the Three Storehouses; it is the Small Vehicle concept of Nirvana as consisting of understanding and the cessation of affliction.

"To be led" refers to the two types of milk products which represent the Vaipulya (curdled milk) and Prajna (butter) Teachings. During these two teachings, one is being led.

"Enter" means to "enter the Buddha's knowledge and
vision." We speak of opening, demonstrating, awakening to,
and entering the Buddha's wisdom. To "rest" refers to the
opening of the Buddha's wisdom. "To be led" refers to the
demonstrating and awakening to the Buddha's wisdom.

"Enter" means to enter the Buddha's wisdom, to open
the provisional and reveal the real, to speak of the Buddha Vehicle and no other vehicles.

Still, with "rest, to be led, and to enter," one has
not yet arrived at the Ultimate Treasure Trove. That is
why this extinction is called a "Transformed City." It is
a provisionally set up expedient device. The Treasure
Trove is the Real Teaching. The Nirvana of the Two Vehicles is merely a Transformed City. It is a provisional
expedient device set up by the Buddha.

This is an explanation according to causes and conditions. Now, to explain it,

2) According to the essentials of the teaching: Those
of the Three Storehouse Teaching, thought of Nirvana as
peace and rest. They thought, "Going to Nirvana is the
greatest! Ahhh!!! There's no trouble there at all. No
affliction. No gossip." So those of the Three Storehouse Teaching really liked the idea of Nirvana. They
wished to cross over into extinction. They viewed the
Three Realms and wanted to be Solitarily Enlightened Ones.
This is like a certain type of person who feels that
everyone else is wrong, and he alone is right. He wants

to go off and live somewhere all by himself thinking
that would be the most wonderful. He feels it's just too
much trouble to be around people.

Bodhisattvas of the Separate Teaching aren't like
that. They think, "You aren't very good? I will draw
closer to you. I will not leave you. I specialize in
crossing over those who do not believe in Buddhism. If
you don't believe in Buddhism, I will influence you some-
how to bring forth the Bodhi mind." This is the state of
a Bodhisattva. The Bodhisattvas and those of the Two Vehicles are direct opposites. Bodhisattvas are like fa-
thers who are out looking for their children, travelling
across a very dangerous road. Suddenly they come to a
very dangerous city. One foot is inside the dangerous
city, and the other is outside. They are well aware that
it is a very dangerous city. V-e-r-y dangerous! But
when they think of their children they forget the danger.
They go right into the dangerous city after them. This is
the Buddha and the Bodhisattvas making vows to come into
the world to save living beings. The Bodhisattva, keeping a few of his old habits--not cutting them all off yet
--goes into birth and death and does not certify to the
doctrine of true emptiness.

The Separate Teaching is the Prajna Period. The Storehouse Teaching is the Agama Period. The Pervasive Teaching
is the Vaipulya Period. The Perfect Teaching is the Lotus
Flower-Nirvana Period. The Separate Teaching calls the

City "The so-called City, which is Like an Illusion." It
is an unreal city used to guard against dangers. The city
is used as an expedient to cut off the delusions of views
and thought. Although the delusions of views and thought
have been cut off, they do not claim this is the highest
state. Therefore, they call it the "so-called City."

They don't claim it is the ultimate state. Those of
the Two Vehicles go ahead and claim that their Nirvana is
the highest state when actually it isn't at all ultimate.
Bodhisattvas purify the Buddhalands, roam and play among
human beings, teaching and transforming living beings.
They realize it isn't the ultimate Dharma.

Those of the Perfect Teaching, the Lotus Flower-Nirvana
Period, know that originally there are no thieves. Since
there are no thieves, they don't want a city, so they call
the city they have a "Transformed City," an unreal city.
This chapter takes it's title from the doctrine of the Perfect Teaching. Thus, it is called "The Analogy of the
Transformed City."

Those of the Three Storehouse and the Pervasive Teaching think that their Nirvana is ultimate. They don't think
of it as a Transformed City. That's the Two Vehicles for
you. Those of the Separate Teaching won't say it's ultimate and they won't admit that it's just a transformation.
That's the state of the Bodhisattva. Those of the Perfect
Teaching, the state of the Buddha, say it is not ultimate;
it is a transformed city.

One may also analyze it from the point of view of the Four Siddhanta, or Four Methods by which the Buddha bestowed the teaching, the first being:

1) Mundane, or ordinary methods of giving: originally, the Transformed City wasn't there. But, suddenly it appeared, and the people who saw it were happy.

2) Individual treatment: when certain individuals gained understanding and rest through the analogy.

3) Diagnosing and treating moral diseases: the City guards against thieves and invaders.

4) Primary truth: in the end, when they gain real extinction.

The Four Siddhantas explained according to the Buddha's response body:

1) The Buddha used the provisional expedient Dharma to set up the City. This is the transforming of the mundane, or ordinary.

2) Living beings brought forth goodness in small measure and this is transforming through individual treatment.

3) Getting rid of the delusions of views and thought is transformation through diagnosis and treatment of moral diseases.

4) In the end, they attain the Great Vehicle and the Great Fruit. This is transformation according to the primary truth.

The Buddha scolded those of the Small Vehicle who

held to their one-sided emptiness. He said that it wasn't in accord with the Middle Way. He told those of the Small Vehicle that they were withered sprouts and sterile seeds, utterly useless. What's to be done? Then he praised the Great Vehicle. He said it was the most wonderful Buddha-dharma. It's the unsurpassed, profound, subtle, wonderful Dharma. He praised the Perfect Teaching as the most wonderful, and he spoke The Wonderful Dharma Lotus Flower Sutra. The doctrine set forth in this Sutra is all perfectly fused without obstruction. It is all inconceivable.

Someone might wonder why, if this Sutra is the Real Teaching, this chapter isn't called "Former Causes and Conditions," Instead of "Transformation City," which is Provisional?

That's a good question. The first part of this chapter does discuss former causes and conditions from many aeons back. Later in the chapter, the analogy of the Transformed City is raised. Bringing up the Transformed City is actually a revelation of the Real Teaching. Those of the Two Vehicles insisted on staying in samadhi all day and refused to move. They stayed in their Nirvana, thinking it very peaceful. They thought they had done what they had to do, finished their great work, and that they would undergo no further becoming. They got stuck in Nirvana and did not make progress in their cultivation. They were attached to Nirvana. Their provisional Dharma was revealed, and they were told it was not right to stay there. They should go forward. That was the purpose of the Transformed City.

At all times, in all places, once you have heard the Buddhadharma, you should not form an attachment to it. Get rid of your attachments.

Sutra: T 262, 22a19

The Buddha told the Bhikshus, "long ago, past limitless, boundless, inconceivable, asankheya aeons, there was a Buddha called Great-Penetrating-Wisdom-Victory, Thus Come One, One Worthy of Offerings, One of Proper and Universal Knowledge, One Whose Understanding and Conduct are Complete, Well-Gone One Who Understands the World, Unsurpassed Lord, Taming and Regulating Hero, Teacher of Gods and Humans, Buddha, World Honored One. His country was named "Good City", and his aeon was named "Great Mark". O Bhikshus, It has been a great, long time since that Buddha passed into extinction.

Outline:

E3. The circuit of speaking the causes and conditions.

F1. Speaking proper of causes and conditions.

1174

> G1. Showing his far-reaching
> knowledge and vision.
>> H1. Prose.
>>> I1. Visible phenomena.

Commentary:

THE BUDDHA TOLD THE BHIKSHUS, Shakyamuni Buddha said
to the Bhikshus... This sentence was added by Ananda when
he compiled the Sutras, LONG AGO, PAST LIMITLESS, BOUND-
LESS, INCONCEIVABLE, ASANKHEYA AEONS, THERE WAS A BUDDHA
CALLED GREAT-PENETRATING-WISDOM-VICTORY. He had great
spiritual penetrations and his wisdom was victorious over
all. So I have told you that where you go you must be
victorious. THUS COME ONE, ONE WORTHY OF OFFERINGS from
gods and humans, OF PROPER AND UNIVERSAL KNOWLEDGE, ONE
WHOSE UNDERSTANDING AND CONDUCT ARE COMPLETE, A WELL-GONE
ONE, WHO UNDERSTANDS THE WORLD. He has gone to the best
place. He is the smartest person in the world. UNSUR-
PASSED LORD. There is no one higher than he is.

> In the heavens and below, there is
>> no one like the Buddha.
> In the ten direction worlds, he is
>> beyond compare.
> Everything in the world--I have
>> seen it all,
> And there's nothing that can compare
>> with the Buddha.

A TAMING AND REGULATING HERO. He can subdue all in the Three Realms. TEACHER OF GODS AND HUMANS, BUDDHA, greatly enlightened one, WORLD HONORED ONE, revered by those in and those beyond the world." Those are the Buddha's ten titles. HIS COUNTRY WAS NAMED "GOOD CITY," because all the citizens were good, not evil, AND HIS AEON WAS NAMED "GREAT MARK." O BHIKSHUS, IT HAS BEEN A GREAT, LONG TIME SINCE THAT BUDDHA PASSED INTO EXTINCTION. How long has it been? He now gives us an analogy:

Sutra: T262, 22a23

Suppose someone were to grind all the earth in the three thousand great thousand worlds into ink powder, and then suppose he passed through a thousand lands to the east and then dropped a particle the size of a mote of dust, and then passing through another thousand lands deposited another mote, and continued to do this until all the ink made of earth was exhausted. What do you think? Could a mathematician or his disciple ever reach the limit of the lands and know their number?

"No, World Honored One."

"O Bhikshus, if the lands this person had

passed through, whether or not he set down a particle in them, were all ground into dust, and if each dust mote was equal to an aeon, then the time since that Buddha passed into extinction would exceed their number by limitless, boundless, hundreds of thousands of tens of thousands of millions of asankheya aeons.

Outline:

> I2. Showing how long it
> was.

Commentary:

"SUPPOSE SOMEONE WERE TO GRIND ALL THE EARTH IN THE THREE THOUSAND GREAT THOUSAND WORLDS INTO INK POWDER, finer than flour, AND THEN SUPPOSE HE PASSED THROUGH A THOUSAND LANDS TO THE EAST AND THEN DROPPED A PARTICLE THE SIZE OF A MOTE OF DUST, AND THEN PASSING THROUGH ANOTHER THOUSAND LANDS, DEPOSITED ANOTHER MOTE, AND CONTINUED TO DO THIS UNTIL ALL THE INK MADE OF EARTH WAS EXHAUSTED. WHAT DO YOU THINK? COULD A MATHEMATICIAN OR HIS DISCIPLE EVER REACH THE LIMIT OF THE LANDS AND KNOW THEIR NUMBER?"

"NO, WORLD HONORED ONE," all the Bhikshus answer.

"O BHIKSHUS, IF THE LANDS THIS PERSON PASSED THROUGH, WHETHER OR NOT HE SET DOWN A PARTICLE IN THEM, WERE ALL GROUND INTO DUST AND IF EACH DUST MOTE WAS EQUAL TO AN

AEON, THEN THE TIME SINCE THAT BUDDHA PASSED INTO EXTINC-
TION WOULD EXCEED THEIR NUMBER BY LIMITLESS, BOUNDLESS,
HUNDREDS OF THOUSANDS OF TENS OF THOUSANDS OF MILLIONS OF
ASANKHEYA AEONS.

The text says, "Suppose someone were to grind all the
earth in the three thousand worlds into ink powder." Now,
just by looking at the ink someone grinds, you can tell
whether his mind is good or bad. If he rubs the stone at
an angle, his mind is not straight, not good. If, when he
writes, he makes a big mess, then his mind is "sick." You
can tell what a person is like by how they grind their ink.
In China, they say, "Grind the ink lightly and hold the
brush firmly." That's the doctrine of grinding ink.

In the T'ang Dynasty there was Li T'ai-po, a poet
from Szechwan. He was very intelligent, but he made a lot
of trouble with his gossip. He knew Kung-fu and swordsman-
ship by the time he was fifteen and was an accomplished
writer by the time he was thirty. Before he was thirty
he went up for the Imperial Examination. There was a pro-
prominent official, Ho Chih-chiang, who was very fond of
him. He told Li T'ai-po, "You are sure to take first
place. I'll speak on your behalf." Now, the heads of the
examining board at that time were Yang Kuo-chung, the elder
brother of Yang Kuei-fei, and Kao Li-shih, a eunuch. Ho
Chih-chiang spoke to them saying, "Li Tai-po really writes
extremely well. He should get the top place." When the
two of them heard this, they were outraged. "You took money

from Li Tai-po as a bribe. We should get a cut! Then
we'll talk about who gets first place! A thousand or two
pounds of gold... do you think you can come here and pull
it off with just your eloquence? Ridiculous!" They thought
that Ho Chih-chiang had received a bribe and withheld their
share. They were very upset. When it came time to draw
straws for writing an article Li T'ai-po got to draw
first. He felt sure that the top place was his and he
felt great. When Yang Kuo-chung saw what he wrote he said,
"With your talent, you're qualified only to grind ink for
me! You're terrible." When Kao Li-shih heard this, he
said, "Grind ink? He isn't good enough to help me put on
my shoes!" Li T'ai-po was so enraged he just stammered,
"All right, fine. See you later," and walked away, without first place, needless to say. Feeling as if he had
really been wronged, he started drinking. He would drink
away his sorrows all day long.

> Li Po wrote a hundred poems with one
> > bottle of wine.
> He slept in the wine shops of Ch'ang-an.
> When the Emperor called, he would not
> > get on the boat;
> He said he was a wine immortal.

From this we can see that in this world, we should
take care not to make anyone too angry at us. If you get
someone too angry at you, you may have to undergo the re-

tribution at any time. Having been insulted so deeply by
Yang Kuo-chung and Kao Li-shih, Li T'ai-po vowed to get
revenge when the chance came. But what chance would he
ever get? He wasn't an official or anybody important. How
would he get his revenge? A chance did come. Not long after the test, a letter came for the Emperor from Korea,
which was written in Korean. Since there was little cul-
tural exchange between countries at that time there were
very few people in China who could read the new Korean lan-
guage. There wasn't anybody, in fact! The Koreans did
this on purpose, to show off to the great country of China
that they couldn't even read that small country's writing.
This would give the Koreans a reason to look down upon the
Chinese. This was a switch, because most countries played
up to China. Anyway, when the Emperor got the letter he
gave it to his officials for a translation but no one
could read it. They all had their Ph.D.s in this and that,
but they couldn't read the letter. The Emperor made it
known that anyone who could read the letter would be ap-
pointed to a high government position, but still, no one
could read it. Li T'ai-po was still staying at Ho Chih-
chiang's house. When Ho Chih-chiang came home with his
eyebrows knitted together in worry, Li T'ai-po asked his
friend, "Why are you so worried?"

Ho Chih-chiang said, "The Koreans have challenged
China. They wrote us a letter which no one can read. It's
in Korean. If we can't even read it, we'll really lose
face. "

Li T'ai-po said, "Can I take a look at it?"

"You know Korean?"

"Sure," smiled Li T'ai-po, "no problem."

"I'll tell the Emperor!" said Ho Chih-chiang, and the next day he did.

The Emperor said, "Well, bring him here! We're looking for just such a person! Why didn't this person take part in the Imperial Examination?"

"He did," said Ho Chih-chiang, "but Yang Kuo-chung and Kao Li-shih refused to give him any recognition."

Li T'ai-po came before the Emperor and agreed to read the letter and write a reply. "I have one condition, however," said Li T'ai-po. "You must ask the Korean envoy to come in person and watch me read the letter and write the reply. That will prove to him that we, in China, have genius among us."

"Of course," the Emperor agreed.

"And another thing," said Li T'ai-po, "after the shabby treatment I got at the examination, I want a special favor."

"Anything you want!" said the Emperor, anxiously.

"While I am doing this, I want Yang Kuo-chung to grind my ink for me and Kao Li-shih to put my shoes on me. When the Koreans see this, they won't know what to think. They'll assume I'm a great talent, and they will thereby respect the country."

"Fine! Fine! This is a special circumstance. That's

a good idea," said the Emperor, and he sent for the two officials. "Yang Kuo-chung," he said, "this is our highest scholar here. You should grind some ink for him." Yang Kuo-chung didn't like the idea, but he had no choice. It was a command from the Emperor. He had said that Li T'ai-po was only good enough to grind his ink, and now he was being forced to grind ink for Li T'ai po!

Kao Li-shih had just been ordered to remove Li T'ai Po's shoes. Seeing this, the envoy thought, "How can Li T'ai-po use such a high official as a servant?" Li T'ai-po asked for some wine, and when he was done drinking, he read the letter and translated it into Chinese for the Emperor. The Korean was amazed. "There's some real talent in China, still," he thought. "We don't dare look down on them."

Li T'ai-po, by this time roaring drunk, then wrote a reply and dismissed the envoy. So that's my story about grinding ink.

Sutra: T. 22b2
Using the power of the Thus Come One's knowledge and vision, I behold that time in the distant past as if it were today.

Outline:

I3. Conclusion: Seeing into the past as if it were the present.

Commentary:

USING THE POWER OF THE THUS COME ONE, the Buddha's, KNOWLEDGE AND VISION, I, Shakyamuni Buddha, SEE INTO THAT TIME IN THE DISTANT PAST AS IF IT WERE TODAY. It doesn't seem too long ago.

Sutra: T. 22b3
At that time, the World Honored One, wishing to restate this meaning, spoke verses, saying,
"I recall that in a past age,
Limitless, boundless aeons ago,
There was a Buddha, doubly honored,
By the name of Great Penetrating
Wisdom Victory.

Outline:

H2. Verse.

I1. Verses about pheno-
mena seen.

Commentary:

AT THAT TIME, THE WORLD HONORED ONE, Shakyamuni Buddha, WISHING TO RESTATE THIS MEANING, SPOKE VERSES, SAYING,
I RECALL THAT IN A PAST AGE/ I remember that in the past,
LIMITLESS, BOUNDLESS AEONS AGO/ How long ago? A very
long time. THERE WAS A BUDDHA, DOUBLY HONORED/ He had

both blessings and wisdom, thus he was doubly honored.

BY THE NAME OF GREAT PENETRATING WISDOM VICTORY/ He had great spiritual penetrations and great wisdom, which were supreme over all.

Sutra: T. 22 b 7

Suppose a person ground
All of the earth that there was
In three thousand great thousand lands
Entirely into ink powder;
And then suppose he passed through a
    thousand lands,
And then let fall one particle of it,
Continuing to drop particles in this way
Until all the ink particles were gone.
Suppose all of the countries he passed
    through,
Whether he dropped particles in them or not,
Again were completely ground into dust
    motes,
And each dust mote were an aeon;
These grains of dust would in number
Be exceeded by the number of aeons
Since that Buddha has passed into
    extinction;
It has been limitless aeons such as this.

1184

Outline:

                         I2. Analogy to clarify
                         the distant past.

Commentary:

    SUPPOSE A PERSON GROUND/ ALL OF THE EARTH THAT THERE WAS/ IN THREE THOUSAND GREAT THOUSAND LANDS/ ENTIRELY TO INK POWDER/ AND THEN SUPPOSE HE PASSED THROUGH A THOUSAND LANDS/ AND THEN LET FALL ONE PARTICLE OF IT/ CONTINUING TO DROP PARTICLES IN THIS WAY/ UNTIL ALL THE INK PARTICLES WERE GONE/ The person passes through a thousand lands and then drops one particle; then he passes through another thousand lands and drops yet another particle, and so on until all the ink is gone. SUPPOSE ALL OF THE COUNTRIES HE PASSED THROUGH/ WHETHER HE DROPPED PARTICLES IN THEM OR NOT/ AGAIN WERE COMPLETELY GROUND INTO DUST MOTES/ AND EACH DUST MOTE WERE AN AEON/ THESE GRAINS OF DUST WOULD IN NUMBER/ BE EXCEEDED BY THE NUMBER OF AEONS/ SINCE THAT BUDDHA HAS PASSED INTO EXTINCTION/ The number of aeons since the Buddha Great Penetrating Wisdom Victory entered extinction exceeds the number of dust motes.

Sutra: T. 22b14

The Thus Come One, with unobstructed wisdom,
Knows of that Buddha's extinction,
And of his sound Hearers and Bodhisattvas,

As if seeing his extinction now.
Bhikshus, you should know
The Buddha's wisdom is pure, subtle, and
*   wondrous;*
Without outflows and without obstructions
It penetrates limitless aeons.

Outline:

> I3. Seeing the past as
> if the present.

Commentary:

THE THUS COME ONE, WITH UNOBSTRUCTED WISDOM/ KNOWS OF
THAT BUDDHA'S EXTINCTION/ of the extinction of the Buddha
Great-Penetrating-Wisdom-Victory, AND OF HIS SOUND HEARERS
AND BODHISATTVAS/ AS IF SEEING HIS EXTINCTION NOW/ Although
it was so long ago, he can see it as if it were happening
right now. BHIKSHUS, YOU SHOULD KNOW/ THE BUDDHA'S WISDOM
IS PURE, SUBTLE, AND WONDROUS/ WITHOUT OUTFLOWS AND WITHOUT
OBSTRUCTIONS/ IT PENETRATES LIMITLESS AEONS/ It penetrates
through those limitless, boundless aeons.

Sutra: T. 22b19

The Buddha told the Bhikshus, "the Buddha
Great-Penetrating-Wisdom-Victory had a life-
span of five hundred forty myriads of millions
of nayutas of aeons."

Outline:

Sutra: T. 22b20

When this Buddha was seated on the
Bodhimanda, having destroyed the troops
of Mara, although he was on the point of
attaining anuttarasamyaksambodhi, still
the Buddhadharmas did not appear before
him. So it was for one minor aeon and then
onwards to ten minor aeons that he sat in the
lotus posture, body and mind unmoving, and
yet the Buddhadharmas still did not appear
before him. Thereupon, the gods of the Triyastrimsha Heaven, spread out for the Buddha,
under a bodhi tree, a lion throne one yojana
in height; on that throne the Buddha was to
attain anuttarasamyaksambodhi. Just as
he sat down upon that throne, the kings of

the Brahma Heavens rained down heavenly flowers over a distance of one hundred yojanas. A fragrant wind from time to time swept away the withered flowers as fresh ones rained down. This continued without interruption for a full ten minor aeons as an offering to the Buddha, the rain of these flowers continuing right up until his extinction. In the same way the gods of the four heavenly kings constantly played heavenly drums as an offering to that Buddha and the other gods made heavenly instrumental music for a full ten minor aeons, right up until his extinction.

Outline:

L2. What happened before he realized the Way.

Commentary:

WHEN THIS BUDDHA WAS SEATED IN THE BODHIMANDA, HAVING DESTROYED THE TROOPS OF MARA, when he went to cultivate and destroy the hordes of demons... When people cultivate, right before they attain the Way, demons come to test them. Do you know how the Buddha became a Buddha? By passing

his tests with demons. A demon manifested a bevy of beautiful women to test the Buddha. Ordinarily in cultivation one may not have much desire, but right before one
accomplishes the Way the big test comes. The heavenly
demons came to destroy the Buddha's Way karma. If the Buddha had even a tiny bit of greed for sex, he would not have
become a Buddha. Since he didn't, he did. Basically, the
women that the demon sent were very beautiful, but the Buddha said, "You may be beautiful now but in thirty, forty,
or fifty years, you will be old, wrinkled, and ugly. You're
just stinking skin bags filled with oozing filth! So much
for all your beauty! Hah!" When the demon women heard
this, they knew that they couldn't disturb his cultivation.
They saw their faces change into the faces of old ladies
with wrinkled skin and bags under their eyes. It was hor-
rible! How could such ugly creatures disturb the Buddha?
So they ran off.

All Buddhas go through pretty much the same testing.
So this Buddha HAVING DESTROYED THE TROOPS OF MARA, AL-
THOUGH HE WAS ON THE POINT OF ATTAINING ANUTTARASAMYAKSAM-
BODHI, enlightenment, STILL THE BUDDHADHARMA DID NOT AP-
PEAR BEFORE HIM, and he wasn't able to certify to the Buddha fruit. SO IT WAS FOR ONE MINOR AEON. An aeon is
396,000 years. A thousand of these is a minor aeon. One
of my disciples was complaining that she had been studying
the Buddhadharma now for two years and still hadn't attained anything! In the larger scheme of things, two years

is like one minute! It's not a long time. This Buddha sat for ONE MINOR AEON AND THEN ONWARDS TO TEN MINOR AEONS, THAT HE SAT IN LOTUS POSTURE, BODY AND MIND UNMOVING. He didn't wriggle around. What's even more difficult, his mind did not even give rise to false thinking. AND YET THE BUDDHADHARMAS STILL DID NOT APPEAR BEFORE HIM. After ten minor aeons, he still hadn't become enlightened and he still hadn't attained the fruit.

THEREUPON, THE GODS OF THE TRIYASTRIMSHA HEAVEN SPREAD OUT FOR THE BUDDHA, UNDER A BODHI TREE, A LION THRONE ONE YOJANA IN HEIGHT; let's say it was a small yojana, that is, forty miles high. ON THAT THRONE THE BUDDHA WAS TO ATTAIN ANUTTARASAMYAKSAMBODHI, the Buddha-fruit. JUST AS HE SAT DOWN UPON THAT THRONE, THE KINGS OF THE BRAHMA HEAVENS RAINED DOWN HEAVENLY FLOWERS OVER A DISTANCE OF ONE HUNDRED YOJANAS, four thousand miles. A FRAGRANT WIND FROM TIME TO TIME SWEPT AWAY THE WITHERED FLOWERS AS FRESH ONES RAINED DOWN. As soon as the petals withered, the breeze blew them away and then new ones rained down. THIS CONTINUED WITHOUT INTERRUPTION FOR A FULL TEN MINOR AEONS AS AN OFFERING TO THE BUDDHA, THE RAIN OF THESE FLOWERS CONTINUING RIGHT UP UNTIL HIS EXTINCTION.

IN THE SAME WAY, THE GODS OF THE FOUR HEAVENLY KINGS CONSTANTLY PLAYED HEAVENLY DRUMS AS AN OFFERING TO THAT BUDDHA, AND THE OTHER GODS MADE HEAVENLY INSTRUMENTAL MUSIC FOR A FULL TEN MINOR AEONS, RIGHT UP UNTIL HIS EXTINCTION.

Sutra: T. 22c2

Bhikshus, the Buddha Great-Penetrating Wisdom-Victory passed through ten minor aeons before the Buddhadharmas finally manifested before him and he attained anuttarasamyaksambodhi.

Outline:

L3. Realizing the Way.

Commentary:

Shakyamuni Buddha told all the great BHIKSHUS, THE BUDDHA GREAT-PENETRATING WISDOM-VICTORY PASSED THROUGH TEN MINOR AEONS BEFORE THE BUDDHADHARMAS FINALLY MANIFESTED BEFORE HIM AND HE ATTAINED ANUTTARASAMYAKSAMBODHI. The Buddhadharmas here refers to enlightenment to the Way, to the attainment of Bodhi, and certifying to the fruit.

Sutra: T. 22c3

Before that Buddha left home he had sixteen sons, the first of whom was named Accumulation of Knowledge. Each of them had a variety of precious, unusual fine toys. When they heard that their father had realized anuttarasam-yaksambodhi they all cast aside these things they valued and went before the Buddha, escorted

by their weeping mothers. Their grandfather,
a Wheel Turning Sage King, together with a
hundred great ministers and with hundreds
of thousands of myriads of millions of citizens
all surrounded them and accompanied them
to the Bodhimanda, all wishing to draw
near to the Thus-Come-One-Great-Penetrating-
Wisdom-Victory, to make offerings to him,
to honor, revere and praise him. When they
arrived, they bowed with their head at his feet,
and having circumambulated him, they single-
mindedly joined their palms, respectfully gazed
upward at the World Honored One, and uttered
these verses:

World Honored One of great and awesome
    virtue,
For the sake of crossing over living beings
After limitless millions of aeons,
You accomplished Buddhahood,
And perfected all your vows;
Unsurpassed is our good fortune.
Very rare you are, World Honored One,
In one sitting, passing through ten minor
    aeons,

With body, hands, and feet,
Still, secure, and unmoving.
Your mind, ever tranquil,
Never knows distraction.
Ultimate, your eternal extinction,
As you dwell firmly in the non-outflow
    dharma.
Now we see the World Honored One
Serenely realize the Buddha Path;
We all gain good benefit
And proclaim our delight and great joy.
Living beings, ever tormented by suffering,
Blind, and without a guide,
Fail to recognize the path which ends that
    pain,
And do not know to seek their liberation.
During the long night the evil destinies
    increase,
While the hosts of gods are reduced in
    number;
From darkness they proceed into darkness,
Never hearing the Buddha's name.
Now, the Buddha's gained the utmost
Peace, rest, the non-outflow way;

And we, and all the gods,
To attain the greatest benefit
Therefore bow our heads
And return our lives to the Unsurpassed
Honored One.

Outline:

L4. Offerings made to him by
his retinue after he realized
the Way.

Commentary:

BEFORE THAT BUDDHA LEFT HOME, HE HAD SIXTEEN SONS, THE
FIRST OF WHOM WAS NAMED ACCUMULATION OF KNOWLEDGE. They had
accumulated all kinds of merit and virtue through their wis-
dom, and so they got to be children of the Buddha. EACH
OF THEM HAD A VARIETY OF PRECIOUS, UNUSUAL, FINE TOYS. Their
grandfather had been a wheel-turning sage king and had bles-
sings as vast as all under heaven. So, the children had
some very precious, unusual, expensive toys. "WHEN THEY
HEARD THAT THEIR FATHER HAD REALIZED ANUTTARASAMYAKSAM-
BODHI, had become a Buddha, THEY ALL CAST ASIDE THESE
THINGS THEY VALUED--they put their toys aside--AND WENT
BEFORE THE BUDDHA, to the Bodhi tree, where the Buddha had
attained enlightenment. ESCORTED BY THEIR WEEPING MOTHERS.
Their mothers, crying and sniffling, took them there.

They had been the Buddha's wives before he left home; now, their only recourse was to cry. They cried over every little thing. The children wanted to go with their father; they didn't want to stay with their mothers.

...THEIR GRANDFATHER, their father's father--A WHEEL TURNING SAGE KING, TOGETHER WITH A HUNDRED GREAT MINISTERS, who were very close to the Sage King, AND WITH HUNDREDS OF THOUSANDS OF MYRIADS OF MILLIONS OF CITIZENS ALL SURROUNDED THEM AND ACCOMPANIED THEM TO THE BODHIMANDA, where the Buddha cultivated the Way, ALL WISHING TO DRAW NEAR TO THE THUS COME ONE GREAT-PENETRATING-WISDOM-VICTORY, TO MAKE OF- FERINGS TO HIM, TO HONOR , REVERE, AND PRAISE HIM. WHEN THEY ARRIVED, THEY BOWED WITH THEIR HEADS AT THE BUDDHA'S FEET. This means that they made a full "five-point" pros- tration, that is, they bowed with their head, their two arms, and their two legs touching the ground. When they bowed down they turned their palms upwards as if the Bud- dha might stand on the palms of their hands. This is called "bowing to receive the Buddha, AND, HAVING CIRCUM- AMBULATED HIM, three times to the right, THEY SINGLEMINDED- LY JOINED THEIR PALMS, RESPECTFULLY GAZED UPWARD AT THE WORLD HONORED ONE, unblinkingly...

They gazed upward because he was sitting up very high; you remember his lion throne was one yojana tall.

Then the entire multitude UTTERED THESE VERSES:

WORLD HONORED ONE OF GREAT AND AWESOME VIRTUE/ The Bud- dha is honored both in and beyond the world. FOR THE SAKE

OF CROSSING OVER LIVING BEINGS/ Why did you decide to become a Buddha? Because you wanted to save living beings.

AFTER LIMITLESS MILLIONS OF AEONS/ YOU ACCOMPLISHED BUDDHA-HOOD/ AND PERFECTED ALL YOUR VOWS/ So those who study the Buddhadharma must make vows. The best day to make vows is on the anniversary of Shakyamuni Buddha's enlightenment, that is, on the eighth day of the twelfth month (lunar calendar). The Buddhas realized Buddhahood through their vows. We want to cultivate; why is it we are unable to endure suffering and unable to be vigorous? We cultivate for two and a half days, but by the time the third day rolls around, we get lazy. The reason for this is because we haven't made vows. We insist on being selfish and seeking our own benefit. We tend towards the Small Vehicle and we think like Arhats. "I'm going to take care of myself, and that's it. If I make it, that's great, but I'm not going to worry about anybody else. I don't care if anybody else cultivates or not. Every move I make is for my own benefit, not for living beings." Very independent. Hah! This is because one hasn't made vows. So, I hope you do make vows.

Vows are very important. But, you can't make someone else's vows. You can't say, "I will make Kuan Yin Bodhisattva's ten vows, or Universal Worthy Bodhisattva's Ten Vows, Amitabha's Forty-eight vows, or Medicine Master's twelve vows." Those are their vows. You can't just copy them. You must make your own vows. You could make vows even greater than Amitabha Buddha or Kuan Yin Bodhisattva, but they must be your own. You aren't them!

"Well," you might argue, "suppose I am a transformation of Amitabha Buddha? What's wrong with making his vows
then?"

Even if you are, you are still just a transformation;
you aren't the original. You have to make new vows. It's
like metal which was one thing and then got melted down into
something else. Perhaps you were a metal sculpture of a
turtle, and now you've turned into a train. You can't be a
turtle again, not even if you want to. I won't argue with
you about whether or not you are Amitabha Buddha's transformation body, but you still need to make brand new vows, not
old ones. There are some old vows which everyone can make;
they are standard vows that every Bodhisattva makes, and
that's all right:

  I vow to save the boundless numbers of beings.

  I vow to cut off the inexhaustible afflictions.

  I vow to study the endless Dharma doors.

  I vow to realize the supreme Buddha Way.

When Amitabha Buddha was on the causal ground, he
was a Bhikshu by the name of Fa-tsang (Dharmakara). He
made forty-eight vows which he used to cultivate with in
every lifetime. He made these vows in every life for who
knows how many great aeons before he became a Buddha and
created the Land of Ultimate Bliss. One should make vows
right at the beginning when you start cultivating. Even

if you are an old-timer and have been cultivating for quite
a while, you should make solid vows. Perhaps some of you
have been planting Buddha-seeds throughout many lifetimes,
many aeons, even, and now as a result you have encountered
this opportunity. You are able to put all of your energy
into practicing the Buddhadharma. So, write out your vows.
You can write them just how you want them. Perhaps: #1: I
vow to save all ants. #2. I vow to save all mosquitoes.
#3. I vow to save all hopeless cases. Of course, I'm jok-
ing. But, one of my disciples did make a vow to become a
Buddha in the northern continent of Uttarakuru. Why did he
do this? Because, right now, there is no Buddha there.
When he gets there, because there are no Buddhas, he will
be worshipped exclusively for sure! Not much competition!
I was quite pleased with this vow; it's very special, so I
made a vow that I would guarantee that he fulfills that vow.
Everything in the world can change. There's nothing fixed.
If someone makes a vow to go somewhere and become a Buddha,
a Buddha will, in the future, appear in that place. No one
ever made a vow to become a Buddha in Uttarakuru before, so
there is no Buddhadharma there right now.

Once you have made the vow, then even if you would
like to slack off on your cultivation, you won't dare, because you made a vow to cultivate! Vows are extremely important.

UNSURPASSED IS OUR GOOD FORTUNE/ VERY RARE YOU ARE,
WORLD HONORED ONE/ IN ONE SITTING, PASSING THROUGH TEN MINOR
AEONS/

WITH BODY, HANDS, AND FEET/ STILL, SECURE, AND UNMOV-
ING/ This praises the Buddha's samadhi in its physical aspect. YOUR MIND, EVER TRANQUIL/ NEVER KNOWS DISTRACTION/
This praises the Buddha's samadhi in its mental aspect. His
mind is free of defilements, and so he is always content
and tranquil. ULTIMATE, YOUR ETERNAL EXTINCTION/ AS YOU
DWELL FIRMLY IN THE NON-OUTFLOW DHARMA/ The Buddha has sev-
ered forever the very roots of delusion and ignorance and
certified to the great extinction. NOW WE SEE THE WORLD
HONORED ONE/ SERENELY REALIZE THE BUDDHA PATH/ WE ALL GAIN
GOOD BENEFIT/ AND PROCLAIM OUR DELIGHT AND GREAT JOY/ LIV-
ING BEINGS, EVER TORMENTED BY SUFFERING/ BLIND, AND WITHOUT
A GUIDE/ FAIL TO RECOGNIZE THE PATH WHICH ENDS THAT PAIN/
AND DO NOT KNOW TO SEEK THEIR LIBERATION/ In their confusion, living beings become bound by suffering. They are as
if blind and without a guide. They don't recognize the path
which leads to the ultimate end of suffering. They don't
know enough to seek to escape.

DURING THE LONG NIGHT, THE EVIL DESTINIES INCREASE/
WHILE THE HOSTS OF GODS ARE REDUCED IN NUMBER/ Beings fall
and are reborn in lower destinies. FROM DARKNESS THEY PRO-
CEED INTO DARKNESS/ NEVER HEARING THE BUDDHA'S NAME/ With
their darkened minds, they create dark karma and receive
retribution.

NOW THE BUDDHA'S GAINED THE UTMOST/ PEACE, REST, THE
NON-OUTFLOW WAY/ Now the Buddha has attained the supreme,
peaceful, quiescent, non-outflow Path of the Sages. AND

WE, AND ALL THE GODS/ TO ATTAIN THE GREATEST BENEFIT/ THERE-
FORE BOW OUR HEADS/ AND RETURN OUR LIVES TO THE UNSURPASSED
HONORED ONE/

    After you Take Refuge and start to cultivate the Way,
you should get rid of your attachment to the mark of a self.
If you don't, you will have not just one kind of trouble, but
many, many kinds. If you can get rid of the mark of a self,
you will have no trouble at all. It's easy to say, "no self."
It's very hard to do. So, you must give up your body, mind,
and life itself to the Buddha in refuge. Life itself: that
is the most important thing we each possess. If you give
your life up to the Buddha, your own personal happiness or
sorrow, or whatever, will cease to be important. We suffer
because we are supposed to suffer, and we enjoy happiness as
it is due. But don't hold on to the idea of a "self." This
is very important in your cultivation.

Sutra: T. 22 c28

When the sixteen sons had finished praising
the Buddha, they then entreated him to turn
the Dharma wheel, saying, "World Honored
One, speak the Dharma and bring us peace,
show us pity, and benefit both gods and humans."
Then they spoke more verses saying:
    " O Hero of the World, incomparable
    Adorned with a hundred blessings,

And having attained unsurpassed wisdom,
Pray speak for the sake of this world
To cross over and liberate us and
All classes of living beings as well.
Demonstrate it: speak it in detail
And lead us to attain that wisdom,
For, if we can attain Buddhahood,
Other living beings can do the same.
The World Honored One knows the profound
   thoughts
Within the minds of living beings;
He knows the ways on which they walk
And the strength of their wisdom,
The pleasures and the blessings they have
   cultivated,
And all the deeds done in former lives.
The World Honored One, knowing all of
   this,
Should turn the unsurpassed wheel !"

Outline:

                   L5. The request to turn the
                   Dharma wheel.

Commentary:

WHEN THEY HAD FINISHED PRAISING THE BUDDHA, THEY
THEN ENTREATED HIM TO TURN THE DHARMA WHEEL, SAYING...
After they had praised the Great Penetration Victory Buddha, they asked him to speak the Dharma. The Buddha will
not speak the Dharma unless requested to do so.

> The Dharma doesn't arise of itself;
> It appears in response to the situation.
> The Way is not practiced in a vacuum;
> It responds in accord with conditions.

Now, before the Dharma lecture, someone always requests the Dharma. If you can't speak the Dharma yourself,
then you ask someone else to do so. In China, when a patron
knows a certain Dharma Master is skilled at lecturing on
the Dharma, he will request him to lecture on a Sutra and
give him a lot of money. In this way, the patron partici-
pates in the merit and virtue generated from the lecturing
of the Sutra.

You may wonder, if the Dharma Master is lecturing on
the Sutra, how can the merit and virtue go to the patron?
It is because of the patron's sincerity in requesting the
Dharma. He requests it not just for himself, but for living beings, and so he gains much merit. Not only does he
gain merit but he receives the reward of intelligence. If
you want to be intelligent then read more Sutras, recite
more Sutras, and request that people lecture on the Sutras

more often. People who are intelligent now did these things
in the past. Those who request the Dharma each day will,
in the future certainly be intelligent and give rise to
Prajna wisdom. The sixteen sons asked the Buddha Great-
Penetrating-Wisdom-Victory to turn the Dharma wheel.

What is meant by "turning the great Dharma wheel?"
Lecturing on the Sutras and speaking the Dharma is turning
the Dharma wheel. Any kind of work that you do within the
Buddhadharma can be considered turning the great Dharma
wheel. There are many different ways to turn the Dharma
wheel. Protecting the Triple Jewel is one; praising the
Triple Jewel is another; propagating the Dharma is another.
Telling people of the benefits of believing in the Buddha is
another.

Let's say a situation arose where some people were
trying to ruin a Dharma Master's reputation. They are
jealous of that Dharma Master and want to break up his Bodhimanda. In this case you should speak up and say, "That's
wrong. These people are just creating rumors. They are
the one's who are destroying the Triple Jewel."

Those people may make up stories and start rumors cir-
culating, saying things like, "That Dharma Master eats
meat," when they have never seen him eat meat at all. If
they had seen him eating meat, that's one thing, but to fab-
ricate stories is just being malicious. They may say, "He
says he eats one meal a day, but he sneaks food all the
time." You should speak up and protect the Triple Jewel

and expose these people as gossip-mongers. That, too, is protecting the Triple Jewel. In general, translating Sutras, lecturing on the Sutras, printing Sutras, running the tape recorder, this is all turning the Dharma wheel.

They said, "'WORLD HONORED ONE, SPEAK THE DHARMA AND BRING US PEACE, SHOW US PITY, AND BENEFIT BOTH GODS AND HUMANS." THEN THEY SPOKE VERSES SAYING:

" O HERO OF THE WORLD, INCOMPARABLE/ ADORNED WITH A HUNDRED BLESSINGS/ The Buddha is a great hero in the world, an unsurpassed lord. There is no one who can compare to the Buddha. He is peerless. The Buddha cultivated blessings and wisdom for three great asankheya aeons, and for a hundred aeons he perfected the fine marks. AND HAVING ATTAINED UNSURPASSED WISDOM/ PRAY SPEAK FOR THE SAKE OF THIS WORLD/ The Buddha is the greatly enlightened one, one with supreme wisdom. PRAY SPEAK FOR THE SAKE OF THIS WORLD/ TO SAVE AND LIBERATE US AND/ so that we may leave suffering and attain bliss--ALL CLASSES OF LIVING BEINGS AS WELL/ all the twelve categories of living beings--DEMONSTRATE IT: SPEAK IT IN DETAIL/ AND LEAD US TO ATTAIN THAT WISDOM/ so all living beings can attain the Buddha's wisdom. FOR, IF WE CAN ATTAIN BUDDHAHOOD/ OTHER LIVING BEINGS CAN DO THE SAME/ If we, now, can become Buddhas, then all living beings can become Buddhas. THE WORLD HONORED ONE KNOWS THE PROFOUND THOUGHTS/ WITHIN THE MINDS OF LIVING BEINGS/ He knows what their hopes and wishes are. AND THE STRENGTH OF THEIR WISDOM/ the scope of their intelligence. THE PLEASURES AND THE

BLESSINGS THEY HAVE CULTIVATED/ AND ALL THE DEEDS DONE IN
FORMER LIVES/ the workings of cause and effect. THE WORLD
HONORED ONE, KNOWING ALL OF THIS/ SHOULD TURN THE UNSUR-
PASSED WHEEL!/ It is our fervent prayer that the World
Honored One will turn the Dharma wheel and save living be-
ings, so they may all realize the Buddha Way.

We are all gathered here to investigate the Buddhadharma, and we should put into practice the knowledge we
gain. If you understand a principle, do not fail to apply
it. If you know and don't practice, that is worse than
not knowing in the first place. If you don't know about
cultivating, and so you don't cultivate, that's one thing.
Once you know about the Buddhadharma, you must cultivate
it, you must practice very reliably and solidly.

The most important job of a cultivator is to benefit
others, to help others. Don't worry about helping yourself. Forget yourself. That's cultivation. It is extremely important not to be jealous or obstructive. You
must also sever affliction. If you don't cut off your afflictions, you won't be able to end birth and death. "Cutting off" afflictions really just means to transform them.
Transform your afflictions into Bodhi. Turning them into
Bodhi, you will always give rise to wisdom, and you won't
be stupid. If you have affliction, then you are always
stupid and without wisdom. Don't get afflicted over every
little thing. Don't be jealous or obstructive. This is
crucial. So, everyday we investigate the Buddhadharma, and

everyday we must practice it.

> You may speak wonderfully, speak just fine;
> But if you don't practice it, it's not
> the Way.

No matter how well you can talk, if you don't actually cultivate you won't be able to realize the Path. There are several people here who are just on the verge of getting enlightened. However, they must cultivate their hearts to benefit others and forget about themselves. Someone is thinking, "Who are they?" Well, if you're wondering who they are, you can be sure they are not you. Besides, you shouldn't ask. You should ask yourself, "When am I going to get enlightened? When am I going to have great wisdom?" You shouldn't ask about the other people. I don't know who they are myself. I just said that to be saying it! I'm not enlightened myself, so how could I know something like that?

The only thing to do is go ahead and cultivate. First of all, be patient. Be patient in all circumstances. Bear up under poverty. Think: "The poorer I am, the better. It's cleaner that way. Cultivators should be poor. Once you get some money, then the problems arrive." Once you've got money, then you won't be able to cultivate. Bear with hunger, too. If there's nothing to eat today, don't worry about it. Something will turn up tomorrow. Be patient. If you have no clothing, if you are freezing, bear it.

1206

Bear the wind and bear the rain. Bear the hunger, bear
the cold. That's your responsibility as a cultivator. You
should fear nothing. No matter how hard it is, you must
do it. "No matter how bitter it is, I must bear it. I will
cultivate and fight against the bitterness and the hardships. I will break through all obstacles." Then, once
you've gotten through that barrier, you can have success.
Otherwise, you won't.

So, every one of you should understand: it is useless
just to talk about it. You have to do it. Talking ten
feet isn't as good as practicing a foot. I hope that all
of you will really practice and that you won't indulge in
intellectual Ch'an.

Sutra: T. 23a11

The Buddha, Shakyamuni, told the Bhikshus,
"When the Buddha-Great-Penetrating-Wisdom-
Victory attained anuttarasamyaksambodhi,
in each of the ten directions, five hundred
myriads of millions of Buddha worlds quaked
in six ways. The dark recesses between those
lands that the awesome light of the sun
and moon could not illumine then were
brightly lit, and the living beings therein were
able to see one another. They all said 'where
have all these living beings come from?' Fur-

ther, in those lands, all the heavenly palaces, up to the Brahma palaces, quaked in six ways. A great light shone everywhere, illumining the entire universe and surpassing the light of the heavens."

Outline:

> K2. Brahma Kings from ten di-
> rections request the Dharma.
>> L1. Awesome light shines and
>> shakes the earth.

Commentary:

THE BUDDHA, SHAKYAMUNI, TOLD THE BHIKSHUS, "WHEN THE BUDDHA, GREAT PENETRATING WISDOM VICTORY, ATTAINED ANNUT-TARASAMYAKSAMBODHI, the utmost right and perfect enlighten-ment, IN EACH OF THE TEN DIRECTIONS, FIVE HUNDRED MYRIADS OF MILLIONS OF BUDDHA WORLDS QUAKED IN SIX WAYS. THE DARK RECESSES BETWEEN THOSE LANDS, THAT THE AWESOME LIGHT OF THE SUN AND MOON COULD NOT ILLUMINE, THEN WERE BRIGHTLY LIT, AND THE LIVING BEINGS THEREIN WERE ABLE TO SEE ONE ANOTHER. THEY ALL SAID, 'WHERE HAVE ALL THESE LIVING BEINGS COME FROM?'" Basically, there weren't any living beings in these dark places. Why are there suddenly living beings there now? Actually, they thought there weren't any liv-ing beings because it was dark, and they couldn't see them. Now it was light and so they were visible.

"FURTHER, IN THOSE LANDS, ALL THE HEAVENLY PALACES,

UP TO THE BRAHMA PALACES, QUAKED IN SIX WAYS. A GREAT
LIGHT SHONE EVERYWHERE, ILLUMINING THE ENTIRE UNIVERSE
AND SURPASSING THE LIGHT OF THE HEAVENS."

Sutra: T. 23 a 18

At that time, in five hundred myriads of millions of lands to the east, the Brahma Heaven palaces shone with a light twice that of their usual brightness. Each of the Brahma Heaven Kings had this thought, "now the palaces are brighter than ever before. What is the reason for this manifestation?"

Outline:

> L2. Brahma Kings come to
> make their request.
>> M1. East.
>>> N1. Startled by
>>> the portents.

Commentary:

AT THAT TIME, IN FIVE HUNDRED MYRIADS OF MILLIONS OF
LANDS TO THE EAST, THE BRAHMA HEAVEN PALACES SHONE WITH A
LIGHT TWICE THAT OF THEIR USUAL BRIGHTNESS. All darkness
was dispersed. Never had they seen such a dazzling display
of light. EACH OF THE BRAHMA HEAVEN KINGS HAD THIS THOUGHT,
"NOW THE PALACES ARE BRIGHTER THAN EVER BEFORE. WHAT IS

THE REASON FOR THIS MANIFESTATION?'"

Sutra: T 23a 20
Then, the Brahma Heaven Kings visited one another and discussed this matter. In the assembly there was one great Brahma Heaven King by the name of Rescuing All, who on behalf of the Brahma hosts spoke verses, saying,
All of our palaces
Are bright as never before;
What is the reason for this?
Let us seek it together.
Is it because a great and virtuous god has been born?
Or because a Buddha has appeared in the world
That this great light
Shines throughout the ten directions?

Outline:

N2. Talking it over among themselves.

Commentary:

THEN, THE BRAHMA HEAVEN KINGS VISITED ONE ANOTHER AND DISCUSSED THIS MATTER. They had a meeting to investigate this question. IN THE ASSEMBLY THERE WAS ONE GREAT BRAHMA HEAVEN KING BY THE NAME OF RESCUING ALL, WHO, ON BEHALF OF THE BRAHMA HOSTS, SPOKE VERSES, SAYING:

ALL OF OUR PALACES/ ARE BRIGHT AS NEVER BEFORE/ WHAT IS THE REASON FOR THIS?/ LET US SEEK IT TOGETHER/ Let's find out why. IS IT BECAUSE A GREAT AND VIRTUOUS GOD HAS BEEN BORN / OR BECAUSE A BUDDHA HAS APPEARED IN THE WORLD/ THAT THIS GREAT LIGHT/ SHINES THROUGHOUT THE TEN DIRECTIONS / Such bright light must surely be an auspicious sign. What does it portend?

Sutra: T. 23a27

At that time, the Brahma Heaven Kings from five hundred myriads of millions of lands, together with their palaces, each with sacks filled with heavenly flowers, went to the west to seek out this manifestation. They saw the Thus Come One Great-Penetrating-Wisdom-Victory seated on the lion throne beneath the Bodhi tree in the Bodhimanda, revered and circumambulated by gods, dragon kings, gandharvas, kinnaras, mahoragas, and beings both human and non-human. They *saw as well the sixteen sons of the king requesting the Buddha to turn the Dharma wheel.*

Outline:

> N3. Following the
> light, they see
> the Buddha.

Commentary:

AT THAT TIME, THE BRAHMA HEAVEN KINGS FROM FIVE HUN-
DRED MYRIADS OF LANDS to the east, TOGETHER WITH THEIR
PALACES... The gods do not ride, like we do, in busses or
airplanes. They ride in their palaces. They can fly
through the air, or travel on the ground. They are sort
of like celestial Winnebagos, complete with every conven-
ience. Riding in them, they can go everywhere they please.
They are even more wonderful than our airplanes. So the
great Brahma heaven kings came with their palaces that they
lived in. EACH WITH SACKS FILLED WITH HEAVENLY FLOWERS,
WENT TO THE WEST TO SEEK OUT THIS MANIFESTATION. THEY SAW
THE THUS COME ONE GREAT-PENETRATING-WISDOM-VICTORY, SEATED
ON THE LION THRONE BENEATH THE BODHI TREE IN THE BODHIMANDA
REVERED AND CIRCUMAMBULATED BY GODS, DRAGON KINGS, GANDHAR-
VAS, KINNARAS, MAHORAGAS, AND BEINGS BOTH HUMAN AND NON-
HUMAN. The gods, dragons, and eightfold division--they
were reverently walking around him. THEY SAW, AS WELL, THE

SIXTEEN SONS OF THE KING, the Wheel Turning King, REQUEST-ING THE BUDDHA, Great-Penetrating-Wisdom-Victory, TO TURN THE DHARMA WHEEL.

Sutra: T. 23 b 2

Then, the Brahma Heaven Kings bowed with their heads at the Buddha's feet, cir-cumambulated him a hundred thousand times, and scattered heavenly flowers upon him. The flowers were piled as high as Mount Sum-eru, and they offered them as well to the Buddha's Bodhi tree, which was ten yojanas in height. Having made offerings of flowers, each presented his palace to the Buddha, saying, 'pray show us pity, and benefit us by accepting and occupying these palaces that we offer you!'

Then the Brahma Heaven Kings, in front of the Buddha, with a single mind and the same voice, spoke verses in praise, saying :

  "World Honored One, you are very rare,
  And difficult to encounter ;
  Complete with limitless meritorious virtues,
  you are able to rescue and protect all creatures.
  Great teacher of gods and humans,
  you who pity all the world

All beings in the ten directions
Receive your beneficence.
We have come from
Five hundred myriads of millions of lands,
Setting aside the bliss of deep Dhyana
    samadhi,
For the sake of making offerings to the Buddha.
Blessings we've gained in former lives
Well ornament our palaces.
Now we offer them to the World Honored
    One,
Only praying you will show mercy and
    accept them.

Outline:

N4. Offerings of

the three karmas.

Commentary:

THEN, THE BRAHMA HEAVEN KINGS BOWED WITH THEIR HEADS AT THE BUDDHA'S FEET, in obeisance, CIRCUMAMBULATED HIM A HUNDRED THOUSAND TIMES, AND SCATTERED HEAVENLY FLOWERS UPON HIM, the flowers they had brought were in cloth bags. THE FLOWERS WERE PILED AS HIGH AS MOUNT SUMERU. "Well," you might wonder, "if the flowers were that many, how could they all fit in their bags?"

They could even fit Mount Sumeru into their bags. You know why? Because their bags are treasures. They might look like ordinary heavenly-flower carry-alls, but you could even fit the three thousand great thousand worlds into them if you needed to. They are "miraculous." Our bags can only be stuffed just so full, but their bags always have room for more. That's because they are treasures. Probably, in former existences the bags were cultivators who were greedy for treasures and were always carting flowers and other treasures around, until finally, through the force of their greed, they turned into bags which could carry Mount Sumeru! You shouldn't try to figure these things out with your ordinary, common understanding, either, because this is an inconceivable type of state.

"If the Buddha was seated on a lion throne that was one yojana tall, and the flowers were as high as Mount Sumeru, which is many, many yojanas high, then did the flowers smother the Buddha so that he couldn't even move?" you wonder. "They aren't heavy, but in such quantities, I would imagine they would weigh quite a bit."

You are too compassionate, really, worrying about the Buddha. The Buddha doesn't want you to worry. Mount Sumeru is Mount Sumeru, and the Buddha's throne is the Buddhas throne. They don't obstruct each other. All those flowers don't get in the way of the Buddha's throne, and the Buddha's throne doesn't obstruct the flowers. That's why we say it's wonderful. Don't try to figure it out with your ordinary mind.

AND THEY OFFERED THEM AS WELL TO THE BUDDHA'S BODHI TREE, WHICH WAS TEN YOJANAS IN HEIGHT. Not only did they make offerings to the Buddha, but they offered their flowers to the Buddha's Bodhi tree, as well. HAVING MADE OFFERINGS OF FLOWERS, EACH PRESENTED HIS PALACE TO THE BUDDHA, SAYING, "PRAY SHOW US PITY AND BENEFIT US BY AC-CEPTING AND OCCUPYING THESE PALACES THAT WE OFFER YOU!" Since they felt that their palaces were the most precious things in the world, and they loved them more than anything else, they gave them to the Buddha.

Sometimes people get very fond of their cars. They may even dream about them at night, dreaming that they give them gas or take care of them. The gods are extremely fond of their palaces. Their palaces can fly, and they can travel by land in them, they can sail through space and ride on the clouds. They are their most prized posses-sions. Now, having met the Buddha, they give up their most cherished palace-cars, and they say, "Buddha, please have mercy on us. Be compassionate and benefit us by accepting the palaces. Accept the palaces and occupy them."

THEN THE BRAHMA HEAVEN KINGS, IN FRONT OF THE BUDDHA, WITH A SINGLE MIND AND THE SAME VOICE, SPOKE VERSES IN PRAISE, SAYING: like singing in unison, they said,

WORLD HONORED ONE, YOU ARE VERY RARE/ AND DIFFICULT

TO ENCOUNTER/ It is extremely hard to meet with a Buddha. It is extremely difficult to encounter the Dharma. It is extremely difficult to meet with the Sangha. Now we have met with the Triple Jewel, the Buddha, the Dharma, and the Sangha, COMPLETE WITH LIMITLESS MERITORIOUS VIRTUES/ The Buddha is endowed with limitless virtues--that is how he became a Buddha. Living beings, also, must have limitless virtues to be able to meet the Buddha.

YOU ARE ABLE TO RESCUE AND PROTECT ALL CREATURES/ GREAT TEACHER OF GODS AND HUMANS/ a great guiding master among the gods and among people, YOU WHO PITY ALL THE WORLD/ You are most compassionate and merciful towards all living beings. ALL BEINGS IN THE TEN DIRECTIONS/ RECEIVE YOUR BENEFICIENCE/ are all benefitted by the Buddha.

WE HAVE COME FROM/ FIVE HUNDRED MYRIADS OF MILLIONS OF LANDS/ SETTING ASIDE THE BLISS OF DEEP DHYANA SAMADHI/ We saw the Buddha's light, and so we left our attachment to our daily meditation--and it was very blissful, indeed.

Before you have attained the bliss of Dhyana samadhi, your cultivation will have its "ups and downs," and may be a bit haphazard. But once you have attained that bliss, nobody could keep you from cultivating! You're like a child eating candy. He eats a piece and then wants another--and another--and another. When he sees candy, he forgets everything and grabs for it. Cultivators who attain the bliss of Dhyana samadhi will want to meditate everyday, for sure. They will insist on it. It won't be

okay to skip meditation anymore, because they like its
flavor. They would rather go without eating than go without meditating. Although this is not a good analogy,
you might even say that it is like being addicted to drugs.
If an addict doesn't get his fix, he starts going through
withdrawal. If the cultivator doesn't get his fix, he
doesn't like it one bit. Before you have gained this
bliss, you won't care that much about meditating, but once
you've gained it, you'll think it is more blissful than
absolutely anything else in the world. The gods sit there
meditating all day long in Dhyana samadhi without getting
up. But now, seeing the light and not understanding where
it came from, they all set aside the bliss of samadhi.
Using their spiritual powers, they went sailing across
millions of lands to find its source. FOR THE SAKE OF MAK-
ING OFFERINGS TO THE BUDDHA/

BLESSINGS WE'VE GAINED IN FORMER LIVES/ WELL ORNAMENT
OUR PALACES/ Because of blessings we cultivated in former
lives, we now have such fine, beautiful, all-purpose pal-
aces, exquisitely adorned and beautiful. NOW WE OFFER THEM
TO THE WORLD HONORED ONE/ our most prized possessions, ONLY
PRAYING YOU WILL SHOW MERCY AND ACCEPT THEM/

Sutra: T. 23b18

At that time, the Brahma Heaven Kings,
having praised the Buddha, said "We only
pray that the World Honored One will turn the

Dharma wheel, crossing over living beings,
opening up the way to Nirvana." Then; all the
Brahma Heaven Kings with one mind and the
same voice, proclaimed these verses :
"Hero of the world, doubly perfect honored one,
   We only pray that you will expound and pro-
      claim the Dharma,
   And through the power of your great com-
         passion and pity
   Cross over suffering and tormented living
      beings.

Outline:

N5. Requesting

the turning of

the Dharma wheel.

Commentary:

AT THAT TIME, THE BRAHMA HEAVEN KINGS, HAVING PRAISED
THE BUDDHA, SAID, "WE ONLY PRAY THAT THE WORLD HONORED ONE
WILL TURN THE DHARMA WHEEL." The Buddha was thinking about
taking a rest but living beings wouldn't hear of it! They
kept asking him to turn the Dharma wheel, to go to work.
Turning the Dharma wheel is the Buddha's work. "CROSSING
OVER LIVING BEINGS, AND OPENING UP THE WAY TO NIRVANA, the
path of non-production and non-extinction." THEN, ALL THE

BRAHMA HEAVEN KINGS, WITH ONE MIND AND THE SAME VOICE, PRO-
CLAIMED THESE VERSES:

"HERO OF THE WORLD, DOUBLY PERFECT HONORED ONE/ Great
hero, both in and beyond the world, you who are complete in
both blessings and wisdom, WE ONLY PRAY THAT YOU WILL EX-
POUND AND PROCLAIM THE DHARMA/ AND, THROUGH THE POWER OF
YOUR GREAT COMPASSION AND PITY/ CROSS OVER SUFFERING AND
TORMENTED LIVING BEINGS/ Through the power of your great
kindness bestow happiness upon living beings, and through
the power of your great compassion relieve them of their
sufferings, taking them from the shore of birth and death
across the massive flow of affliction and agony to the
other shore of Nirvana.

Sutra: T. 23 b 22
Thereupon, the Thus Come One Great
Penetrating Wisdom Victory, assented by
his silence.

Outline:

N6. Thus Come One
assents by silence.

Commentary:

THEREUPON, THE THUS COME ONE, GREAT PENETRATING WIS-
DOM VICTORY, ASSENTED BY HIS SILENCE. When the Brahma
Heaven Kings came from the east and requested him to speak
the Dharma, he assented by keeping silent. By not speaking,

he indicated that he would speak Dharma.

Sutra: T. 23 b 22

Furthermore, O Bhikshus, to the southeast the great Brahma Kings in five hundred myriads of millions of lands, seeing their palaces in dazzling brilliance as never before, jumped for joy, thinking it rare indeed.

Outline:

> M2. Southeast.
>
> > N1. Seeing the por-
> > tents in surprise.

Commentary:

FURTHERMORE, O BHIKSHUS, TO THE SOUTHEAST THE GREAT BRAHMA KINGS IN FIVE HUNDRED MYRIADS OF MILLIONS OF LANDS, SEEING THEIR PALACES IN DAZZLING BRILLIANCE AS NEVER BEFORE, JUMPED FOR JOY, THINKING IT RARE INDEED. They saw their palaces lit up as never before. They were exceedingly happy. It was something they had never seen before.

Sutra: T. 23 b 26

They visited one another and discussed this matter. Then, in the assembly, a

Brahma Heaven King by the name of Great
Compassion, on behalf of the Brahma hosts
spoke these verses:
"What is the reason for this event?
Why has this sign appeared?
All of our palaces
Are aglow as never before.
Has a greatly virtuous god been born?
Or has a Buddha appeared in the world?
We have never seen such signs before.
With one mind we should investigate it,
Passing through a thousand myriads of
   millions of lands,
Searching for the light, investigating it
   together.
It must be that a Buddha has appeared
To take across the suffering living beings.

Outline:

N2. Talking it
over among them-
selves.

Commentary:

THEY VISITED ONE ANOTHER AND DISCUSSED THIS MATTER.
They got together and talked it over. THEN, IN THE ASSEM-

BLY, A BRAHMA HEAVEN KING BY THE NAME OF GREAT COMPASSION, ON BEHALF OF THE BRAHMA HOSTS, SPOKE THESE VERSES:

WHAT IS THE REASON FOR THIS EVENT / WHY HAS THIS SIGN APPEARED / ALL OF OUR PALACES/ ARE AGLOW AS NEVER BEFORE/ We have never seen such light! HAS A GREATLY VIRTUOUS GOD BEEN BORN / OR HAS A BUDDHA APPEARED IN THE WORLD / WE HAVE NEVER SEEN SUCH SIGNS BEFORE/ WITH ONE MIND WE SHOULD INVESTIGATE IT/ We should concentrate our efforts to figure out where this light is coming from. PASSING THROUGH A THOUSAND MYRIADS OF MILLIONS OF LANDS/ SEARCHING FOR THE LIGHT, INVESTIGATING IT TOGETHER/ IT MUST BE THAT A BUDDHA HAS APPEARED/ TO TAKE ACROSS THE SUFFERING LIVING BEINGS/ all suffering, miserable living beings.

Sutra: T. 23 c4

At that time, five hundred myriads of millions of Brahma Heaven Kings, together with their palaces, each with sacks filled with heavenly flowers, went to the southwest to seek out this manifestation. They saw the Thus-Come-One Great-Penetrating-Wisdom-Victory seated on the lion throne beneath the Bodhi tree in the Bodhimanda, revered and circumambulated by gods, dragon kings, gandharvas, kinnaras, mahoragas, and beings both human and non-human. They saw, as well, the sixteen sons of the king requesting the Buddha to turn the Dharma wheel.

Outline:

> N3. Following the
> light, they see
> the Buddha.

Commentary:

AT THAT TIME, FIVE HUNDRED MYRIADS OF MILLIONS OF BRAHMA HEAVEN KINGS, from the southeast, TOGETHER WITH THEIR PALACES, EACH WITH SACKS FILLED WITH HEAVENLY FLOW-ERS... The gods are fond of flowers, and so they use them to make offerings to the Buddha, putting them in their cloth flower bags. They WENT TO THE SOUTHWEST TO SEEK OUT THIS MANIFESTATION. THEY SAW THE THUS-COME-ONE GREAT-PENETRATING-WISDOM-VICTORY SEATED ON THE LION THRONE BE-NEATH THE BODHI TREE IN THE BODHIMANDA, way up in the north-west. REVERED AND CIRCUMAMBULATED BY GODS, DRAGON KINGS, GANDHARVAS, KINNARAS, MAHORAGAS, AND BEINGS BOTH HUMAN AND NON-HUMAN. THEY SAW, AS WELL, THE SIXTEEN SONS OF THE KING REQUESTING THE BUDDHA TO TURN THE DHARMA WHEEL.

Sutra: T. 23 c 9

Then the Brahma Heaven Kings bowed with their heads at the Buddha's feet, cir-

cumambulated him a hundred thousand
times, then scattered heavenly flowers upon
him. The flowers were piled as high as
Mount Sumeru, and they offered them as
well to the Buddha's Bodhi tree. Having
made offerings of flowers, each presented
his palace to the Buddha saying, "Show us
pity and benefit us by accepting and occupying these palaces that we offer you!" Then
the Brahma Heaven Kings, before the
Buddha, with a single mind and the same
voice, spoke verses in praise, saying,

" Sagely Lord, king among gods,
   With the kalavinka sound,
   To you who pity living beings,
   We now reverently bow.
   The World Honored One is most rare,
   Appearing but once in long ages.
   One hundred and eighty aeons have
      passed
   Empty, without a Buddha.
   The three evil paths are full.
   The hosts of gods decrease.
   Now the Buddha has appeared in the

world,
To act as eyes for living beings,
As a refuge for the world,
Rescuing and protecting all creatures,
A father for all beings,
Pitying and benefitting them.
Now, through blessings gained in former
*   lives,*
We are enabled to meet the World Honored
*   One.*

Outline:

N4. Three karmas

as an offering.

Commentary:

In this passage, the Brahma gods from the southeast make offerings to the Buddha in just the same way as did the Brahma gods from the east. They, too, presented the Buddha with their most prized possessions, their palaces, and spoke verses to praise the Buddha, saying,

SAGELY LORD, KING AMONG GODS/ WITH THE KALAVINKA SOUND/ The Buddha is called the Sagely Lord, the Sage among Sages, the god among gods. He has the kalavinka sound. In The Amitabha Sutra we read about the kalavinka birds in the Land of Ultimate Bliss. Kalavinka means "fine sounding

bird." Ultimately, how fine they sound you will know when
you hear one. You still don't know how fine they sing.
Once you get to the Land of Ultimate Bliss, then you will
know. The Buddha speaks the Dharma with a sound even finer
than that of the kalavinka bird, so the sound of his voice
is described as the "kalavinka sound." TO YOU WHO PITY
LIVING BEINGS/ The Buddha is most compassionate. WE NOW
REVERENTLY BOW/

THE WORLD HONORED ONE IS MOST RARE/ APPEARING BUT ONCE
IN LONG AGES/ ONE HUNDRED AND EIGHTY AEONS HAVE PASSED/
EMPTY, WITHOUT A BUDDHA/ THE THREE EVIL PATHS ARE FULL/
The hells, the animal realm, and the realm of the ghosts
get increasingly fuller, and THE HOSTS OF GODS DECREASE/
The three evil paths are doing great business! Everyone
wants to live in them! On the other hand, the three good
paths are going bankrupt. NOW THE BUDDHA HAS APPEARED IN
THE WORLD/ TO ACT AS EYES FOR LIVING BEINGS/ Why did everyone end up in the three evil paths? Because they couldn't
tell right from wrong, black from white, good from evil.
They had no one to be their guide, "to act as eyes" for
them. They were in darkness, running in confusion, running
into the three evil paths. Now that the Buddha has. appeared in the world, it is as if living beings had eyes.
Now, the three evil paths can decrease and the three good
paths increase. AS A REFUGE FOR THE WORLD/ All beings in
the world return in refuge to the Buddha and head toward
the good Bodhi path. RESCUING AND PROTECTING ALL CREA-

TURES/ A FATHER FOR ALL BEINGS/ The Buddha cherishes all beings. He is a compassionate father to them. Living beings are like the Buddha's unfilial children. The more unfilial they are, the harder he works to save them. PITYING AND BENEFITTING THEM/ He shows them mercy and benefits them through his great, enlightened compassion. NOW, THROUGH BLESSINGS GAINED IN FORMER LIVES/ WE ARE ENABLED TO MEET THE WORLD HONORED ONE/ We gods, no doubt, in former lives created merit and virtue by doing good deeds, and so now we are lucky enough to meet with the Buddha. We are lucky enough to meet with the Buddha and listen to him speak the Dharma. This is because of good roots planted in former lives.

Sutra: T. 23 c 24

At that time, the Brahma Heaven Gods, having praised the Buddha, said, "We only pray that the World Honored One will take pity on all beings and turn the Dharma wheel to liberate living beings."

Then, the Brahma Heaven Kings, with one mind and a single voice, spoke verses saying,

"Great Sage, turn the Dharma wheel,
To reveal the marks of all Dharmas,
To cross over tormented living beings,

So they may gain great joy.
When living beings hear the Dharma,
They may gain the way, or be reborn in
* the heavens;*
The evil paths will decrease
And those of patience and goodness will
* increase.*

Outline:

> N5. Requesting the
> turning of the
> Dharma wheel.

Commentary:

AT THAT TIME, THE BRAHMA HEAVEN GODS, HAVING PRAISED
THE BUDDHA, in verses, SAID, "WE ONLY PRAY THAT THE WORLD
HONORED ONE WILL TAKE PITY ON ALL BEINGS "and rescue them.
In order to rescue them, he must speak the Dharma, TURN THE
DHARMA WHEEL TO LIBERATE LIVING BEINGS, teaching and trans-
forming them. In this way they can leave suffering, attain
bliss, and put an end to birth and death.

THEN, THE BRAHMA HEAVEN KINGS, WITH ONE MIND AND A
SINGLE VOICE, SPOKE VERSES SAYING --they had different
mouths, but they spoke in unison,

GREAT SAGE, TURN THE DHARMA WHEEL/ TO REVEAL THE MARKS
OF ALL DHARMAS/ to instruct us in the real marks of all
dharmas, in the doctrine of the Dharma. TO CROSS OVER TOR-

MENTED LIVING BEINGS/ all the miserable living beings, SO
THEY MAY GAIN GREAT JOY/

WHEN LIVING BEINGS HEAR THE DHARMA/ that the Buddha
speaks, they can leave suffering and attain bliss and end
birth and death. THEY MAY GAIN THE WAY, OR BE REBORN IN THE
HEAVENS/ Perhaps they certify to the fruition of sagehood,
or perhaps they are born in the heavens. THE EVIL PATHS
WILL DECREASE/ If they are born in the good paths, then the
good paths increase in number and the evil paths decrease,
AND THOSE OF PATIENCE AND GOODNESS WILL INCREASE/ People who
practice forbearance and who do the ten good deeds will increase in number.

Sutra: T. 24 a 2
At that time, the Thus-Come-One Great
Penetrating-Wisdom-Victory assented by his
silence.

Outline:

> N6. Thus Come One
> assents through
> silence.

Commentary:

AT THAT TIME, THE THUS-COME-ONE GREAT-PENETRATING-
WISDOM-VICTORY ASSENTED BY HIS SILENCE. He didn't say anything, and that meant he agreed to speak.

Sutra: T. 24 a 2

Furthermore, O Bhikshus, to the south, the great Brahma Kings in five hundred myriads of millions of Buddhalands, seeing their palaces in dazzling brilliance as never seen before, jumped for joy, thinking it rare indeed.

Outline:

> M3. South.
>> N1. Startled by the portents.

Commentary:

FURTHERMORE, O BHIKSHUS, TO THE SOUTH, THE GREAT BRAHMA KINGS IN FIVE HUNDRED MYRIADS OF MILLIONS OF BUDDHALANDS, SEEING THEIR PALACES IN DAZZLING BRILLIANCE AS NEVER SEEN BEFORE, JUMPED FOR JOY, seeing such light, they were very happy, THINKING IT RARE INDEED, very, very rare.

Sutra: T. 24 a 5

Thereupon, they visited one another and discussed this matter, wondering," why do our palaces glow with the light ?" Then, in the assembly a Brahma Heaven King called Wonderful Dharma, on behalf of the Brahma hosts, spoke these verses,

"All of our palaces
Shine with awesome brilliance;
This cannot be for no reason;
We should seek out this sign.
In a hundred thousand aeons,
Such a sign has never been seen.
Has a great and virtuous god been born?
Or has a Buddha appeared in the world?

Outline:

> N2. Talking it
> over among them-
> selves.

Commentary:

THEREUPON, THEY VISITED ONE ANOTHER AND DISCUSSED THIS MATTER, they had a meeting, WONDERING, "WHY DO OUR PALACES GLOW WITH THE LIGHT?" THEN, right in the middle of the meeting there was A BRAHMA HEAVEN KING, CALLED WONDERFUL DHARMA, who, ON BEHALF OF THE BRAHMA HOSTS, SPOKE THESE VERSES,

ALL OF OUR PALACES/ where we live, SHINE WITH AWESOME BRILLIANCE/ such as we have never seen before. THIS CANNOT BE FOR NO REASON/ There must certainly be a special reason for this light. WE SHOULD SEEK OUT THIS SIGN/ We shouldn't just let it go by; we should find out where it's coming

1232

from. IN A HUNDRED THOUSAND AEONS/ SUCH A SIGN HAS NEVER
BEEN SEEN/ During the past hundred thousand aeons, we haven't
seen such a sign. HAS A GREAT AND VIRTUOUS GOD BEEN BORN?/
OR HAS A BUDDHA APPEARED IN THE WORLD?/ So they all set out
to find the source of the light.

Sutra: T. 24 a 12

At that time, five hundred myriads of millions of Brahma Heaven Kings, together with
their palaces, each with sacks filled with heavenly flowers, went to the north to seek out this
manifestation. They saw the Thus-Come-
One Great-Penetrating-Wisdom-Victory
seated on the lion throne beneath the Bodhi
tree in the Bodhimanda, revered and circumambulated by gods, dragon kings,
gandharvas, kinnaras, mahoragas, and
beings both human and non-human. They saw,
as well, the sixteen sons of the king requesting
the Buddha to turn the Dharma wheel.

Outline:

N3. Following the
light, they see
the Buddha.

Commentary:

AT THAT TIME, FIVE HUNDRED MYRIADS OF MILLIONS OF
BRAHMA HEAVEN KINGS, having praised the Buddha... Brahma
Kings have come from five hundred myriads of millions of
lands to the east, from five hundred myriads of millions of
lands to the southeast, and from five hundred myriads of
millions of lands to the south. TOGETHER WITH THEIR PALACES.
Wherever they went, they rode in their palaces. We have mo-
bile homes, and such, that one can travel in, but they are
usually very small and cramped. The palaces are quite comfortable and can go anywhere.

EACH WITH SACKS FILLED WITH HEAVENLY FLOWERS... The
gods love flowers and incense and never travel without them.
They adorn their palaces with them; the flowers and incense
appear as their rightful enjoyments, the rewards from their
former good deeds. Wherever they go, they carry sacks full
of flowers. They WENT TO THE NORTH TO SEEK OUT THIS MANI-
FESTATION. They hopped into their palaces and headed north
to find the source of the light. THEY SAW THE THUS-COME-ONE
GREAT-PENETRATING-WISDOM-VICTORY SEATED ON THE LION THRONE
BENEATH THE BODHI TREE IN THE BODHIMANDA. They saw that
the light was coming from the Buddha. REVERED AND CIRCUM-
AMBULATED BY GODS, DRAGON KINGS, from the four seas, GANDHAR-
VAS, KINNARAS, MAHORAGAS, AND BEINGS BOTH HUMAN AND NON-
HUMAN.

Gandharvas and kinnaras are music spirits in the court
of the Jade Emperor. Gandharva means "incense inhalers,"

because they love the smell of incense. When the Jade Emperor wants some music, he just lights some incense, and the gandharvas come flying in. Once they get there, the Jade Emperor says, "You make great music. Why don't you play a few tunes for me?" Since they love the incense, they obey the Jade Emperor and make music for him, sniffing the incense all the while.

Kinnara means "doubtful spirit," because they resemble human beings, except that they have a horn on their heads. When they play music and dance for the Jade Emperor, they shake their heads back and forth and around and around, to show off their beautiful horns. At least, they think they are beautiful. They sing, play music, dance, and shake their heads. This all just means that they have no samadhi power! Hah!

The entire eight-fold division is represented in this line of text. They are all very strange. Some have one leg, and some have three legs, and some, like the mahoragas, just crawl on their bellys. Some fly in the sky like the garudas and the musical spirits. The gandharvas and the kinnaras work out of the same union, and, if the Jade Emperor calls in the kinnaras, they will usually demand that the gandharvas be hired, as well, so they can jam together --rocking out on the drums, the conch shells, and the gongs and bells. The I-Ching, The Book of Changes, says, "It appears as an archetype in heaven, and it manifests in the phenomenal on earth," and so we find music groups and musical instruments among people. Why do we have these music groups and these kinds of musical instruments? It's because some people who had their (five) eyes opened took a look into the heavens and saw, "Oh, wow, look at those instruments! Let's make some like that!" and so the great treasury of musical science was opened, thanks to the kinnaras and the ghandharvas. This isn't too hard to figure out. People have pretty much imitated the way things are in heaven.

All the living beings were revering the Buddha, walking around him slowly, keeping him to the right. THEY SAW, AS WELL, THE SIXTEEN SONS OF THE KING REQUESTING THE BUDDHA TO TURN THE DHARMA WHEEL. The sixteen sons of the Buddha were asking him to turn the Dharma wheel. They were the sons of the Buddha not just in one lifetime you might say that in every life they had received the Buddha's teaching and been his Dharma protectors. This life, when the Buddha became a Buddha, they vowed to be his sons and ask him to turn the Dharma wheel. They did this because of their vows. People's relationships to each other work the same way. Each family has its own set of cause and effect. Each country has its own set of cause and effect. People's relationships are based on their mutual cause and effect. In the distant past, the Buddha taught living beings; he taught them for a long time, life after life, being so good to them that they realized, "He is our great compassionate father." They vowed in every life to follow that Buddha, saying, "When you become a Buddha, we will follow you and be your disciples. We will do this in every life. In every life, we will be the Buddha's disciples." They did this before he even became a Buddha. Now that Great-Penetrating-Wisdom-Victory has become a Buddha, the sixteen sons, because of their former vows naturally come and ask him to turn the great wheel of the Dharma.

Sutra: T. 24 a 17

Then the Brahma Heaven Kings bowed with their heads at the Buddha's feet, circumambulated him a hundred thousand times and scattered heavenly flowers upon him. The flowers were piled as high as Mount Sumeru, and they offered them, as well to the Buddha's Bodhi tree. Having made offerings of flowers, each presented his palace to the Buddha, saying, "Show us pity and benefit us by accepting and occupying these palaces that we offer you." Then the Brahma Heaven Kings, before the Buddha, with a single mind and the same voice, spoke verses in praise, saying,

Outline:

N4. Three karmas
as an offering.

Commentary:

THEN THE BRAHMA HEAVEN KINGS BOWED WITH THEIR HEADS AT THE BUDDHA'S FEET, CIRCUMAMBULATED HIM A HUNDRED THOUSAND TIMES... When we circumambulate, it might take one or two minutes to walk around the Buddha just a few times. The gods, however, can walk around the Buddha a hundred thousand times in less than a minute. They use their spiritual powers Don't worry about them, thinking, "If they go around the Buddha a hundred thousand times, how will they have time to listen to the lecture? The lecture takes two hours!" It takes them but a moment. This just shows you, you shouldn't try to figure these things out with your ordinary intelligence.

...AND SCATTERED HEAVENLY FLOWERS UPON HIM, like snow falling upon the Buddha. "THE FLOWERS WERE PILED AS HIGH AS MOUNT SUMERU, the heap of flowers was that high. AND THEY OFFERED THEM, AS WELL, TO THE BUDDHA'S BODHI TREE. Not only did they make offerings to the Buddha, but also to his Bodhi Tree.

You're thinking, "These Brahma gods are too much. Why are they making offerings to a tree? I can see making offerings to the Buddha, but what's the use of making offerings to a tree?"

You should know that the Buddha realized Buddhahood

under the Bodhi tree. It provided him with the space for
becoming a Buddha and thereby gained great merit and virtue. The Great Brahma Kings aren't doing this because they
are stupid, you know, but because they want to thank the
Bodhi tree for helping the Buddha realize Buddhahood. When
the Buddha sat beneath that tree he was sheltered from
the rain, he was cool in the shade, and, best of all, he
became a Buddha. So they make offerings to the Bodhi
tree.

HAVING MADE OFFERINGS OF FLOWERS, EACH PRESENTED HIS
PALACE TO THE BUDDHA... They gave that thing they most
cherished, that thing they could not put down. When they
got born in the heavens they got to live in it. They were
entitled to it as a reward for their past good deeds. It
was inconceivably wonderful. Now they give away what they
could not give away.

The gods don't have anything else to speak of. They
aren't like people who may accumulate a lot of land and
other holdings. They simply possess their palaces and
that's it. There's no "land" in the heavens; there's no
real estate. The heavens are up in empty space! Their
palaces sit in space. And they don't have to use money.
The gods aren't like us, buying, selling, and huckstering.
They don't have land or any possessions other than their
palaces and their flowers. First, they offered their flowers, but then they thought that probably wasn't showing
enough sincerity. "Now that we have met the Buddha, why

not do it right and give him our palaces?" And so they did! Now they had no place to live. I don't know what they planned to do about that, where they were planning to immigrate to.

...SAYING,"SHOW US PITY AND BENEFIT US BY ACCEPTING AND OCCUPYING THESE PALACES THAT WE OFFER YOU. We are singleminded in our desire that the Buddha be compassionate towards us and accept these palaces we offer you. Don't stay there under the Bodhi tree. It's not nearly as luxurious as our palaces. "

THEN THE BRAHMA HEAVEN KINGS, BEFORE THE BUDDHA, WITH A SINGLE VOICE... Now, that's not easy! Just look at translating Sutras, you want to translate it that way, he wants to translate it another way, and someone else has yet another idea about how it should be done. Even if you come to an agreement, there's still a lot of give and take involved, and you are not all of the "same mind." The Great Brahma Heaven Kings all had the same mind, and, not only that, they said the same thing at exactly the same time and SPOKE VERSES IN PRAISE of the Thus-Come-One Great-Penetrating-Wisdom-Victory, SAYING...

Sutra : T. 24 a 23
 "The World Honored One is very hard
     to meet;
 He who breaks through all afflictions.

> "Passing through a hundred and thirty
> aeons,
> Only now do we get to see him.
> May living beings, starving and thirsty,
> Be filled with the rain of Dharma.
> He, whom we have never seen before,
> One of unlimited wisdom,
> Rare as the Udumbara blossom
> Today, at last we have met.
> All of our palaces
> Receiving your light, are adorned.
> In your great compassion, World Honored
> One
> Pray accept and live with them."

Commentary:

    With a single mind and the same sound, the Brahma Kings praised the Buddha. They had the same thought, the same wisdom, the same sound, and the same inconceivable state. That's why they said, THE WORLD HONORED ONE IS VERY HARD TO MEET/ It is extremely hard to meet up with the Buddha. Not only that, it is very rare even to see a Buddha image. For example, in America just a hundred years ago there were no Buddha images. HE WHO BREAKS THROUGH ALL AFFLICTIONS/ The Buddha has already broken through all afflictions, and be-

cause he is greatly compassionate, he breaks through others'
afflictions for them. Not only does he break through his
own, but he wishes to relieve all living beings of their
troubles and afflictions. Someone is afraid, now, thinking,
"My afflictions are so dear to me. I don't want to break
through them," and, they open the door and run out! They
don't want to listen to the Sutra lectures and they don't
want to break through their afflictions. Hah! "If the Buddha broke through my afflictions, I wouldn't know what to
do with myself! That will never do." They think their afflictions are more important than their daily bread.

PASSING THROUGH A HUNDRED AND THIRTY AEONS/ The Brahma Kings from the southwest had passed through a hundred
and eighty aeons, but the Brahma Kings from the south had
only passed through a hundred and thirty aeons, before they
got to see the Buddha. ONLY NOW DO WE GET TO SEE HIM/

MAY LIVING BEINGS, STARVING AND THIRSTY/ Living beings in the three evil ways are said to be hungry and
thirsty. BE FILLED WITH THE RAIN OF DHARMA/ May the rain
of Dharma all at once saturate these parched and hungry
living beings. HE, WHOM WE HAVE NEVER SEEN BEFORE/ They
had never seen the Buddha, heard the Dharma, or met the
Sangha. ONE OF UNLIMITED WISDOM/ The Buddha has limitless, boundless great wisdom and compassion. RARE AS THE
UDUMBARA BLOSSOM/ I have already told you about the udumbara flower. If you want to know what it is, look it up
in your notes. I'm not going to tell you now. Someone

says, "Maybe you forgot!" Well, maybe I did, but you are going to have to remember it! Tomorrow I'm going to ask you what it is, and if you can't answer, then I'm not going to lecture to you anymore. Did you hear?

TODAY, AT LAST, WE HAVE MET/ The Buddha is like the udumbara flower which blooms only once in a great, long while.

ALL OF OUR PALACES/ our most prized possessions, our most beautiful possessions. The things we cannot put down! Our favorite things! Our palaces!!! Now, having met the Buddha, we are going to renounce that which we cannot renounce. RECEIVING YOUR LIGHT, ARE ADORNED/ In the Buddha's light, the palaces appear especially ornate and beautiful. We give them to the Buddha now, and IN YOUR GREAT COMPASSION, WORLD HONORED ONE/ PRAY ACCEPT AND LIVE IN THEM/ Accept our offering to you, so that we may plant blessings and grow in wisdom.

Sutra: T. 24 b1

At that time, the Brahma Heaven Kings, having praised the Buddha, said, "we only pray that the World Honored One will turn the Dharma wheel, causing the entire world with its gods, maras, Brahmans, shramanas, all to become peaceful and calm and to attain liberation." Then, the

Brahma Heaven Kings, with a single mind and the same voice, spoke verses in praise, saying,

" Honored One among gods and humans,
Pray turn the unsurpassed wheel of
Dharma.
Beat upon the Dharma drum,
And blow the great Dharma conch,
Let fall everywhere the great Dharma
rain,
To cross over limitless living beings.
We all beseech you to expound and proclaim
The profound, far reaching sound.

Outline:

N5. Requesting the
turning of the
Dharma wheel.

Commentary:

AT THAT TIME, THE BRAHMA HEAVEN KINGS, HAVING PRAISED
THE BUDDHA, SAID, "WE ONLY PRAY THAT THE WORLD HONORED ONE
WILL TURN THE DHARMA WHEEL, the wonderful wheel of Dharma,
CAUSING THE ENTIRE WORLD WITH ITS GODS, MARAS, BRAHMANS,
SHRAMANAS, left-home people who diligently cultivate moral-
ity, samadhi, and wisdom and eradicate greed, hatred, and

stupidity, ALL TO BECOME PEACEFUL AND CALM AND TO ATTAIN
LIBERATION, to be delivered from the sufferings of the three
evil paths. THEN, THE BRAHMA HEAVEN KINGS, WITH A SINGLE
MIND AND THE SAME VOICE, SPOKE VERSES IN PRAISE, SAYING,
HONORED ONE AMONG GODS AND HUMANS/ PRAY TURN THE UNSUR-
PASSED WHEEL OF DHARMA/ The Buddha is honored in and beyond
the world. We only pray that you will turn the unsurpassed
great wheel of Dharma. BEAT UPON THE DHARMA DRUM/ AND BLOW
THE GREAT DHARMA CONCH/ Before the Dharma is spoken, before ceremonies, or before we start translating, we beat the
drums and bells. Don't think they can't hear it in the heavens. They do! They hear it and think, "Oh, they're going
to work, there, in San Francisco; they are translating! And,
unseen by ordinary people, they stop by to see how the work
is going, "Hmm...are they translating correctly? Are they
just goofing off?" So, don't think you can get away with
anything!!

In the Forty-two Hands, there is a Jeweled Conch Hand.
When you blow the jeweled conch, it fills space and the
Dharma Realm.

LET FALL EVERYWHERE THE GREAT DHARMA RAIN/ Speaking the
Dharma for the benefit of all beings, TO CROSS OVER LIMIT-
LESS LIVING BEINGS/ There are a great many living beings. If
I had been translating these two lines, I would have said,

LET FALL EVERYWHERE THE GREAT DHARMA RAIN,
AND EVERYWHERE SAVE GREAT LIVING BEINGS!

But, the text, as it stands, is okay, too.

Why do I want to change the line to read, "And everywhere save great living beings?" Because living beings, in the future, all can become Buddhas. Everyone is really very great. If I had said, "And everywhere save insignificant living beings," people would have assumed that they were very small and wouldn't cultivate. Great living beings can, in the future, realize the great Buddha Way. That's the way I would have translated it, but it's already been done the other way, and it can't be changed now!

WE ALL BESEECH YOU TO EXPOUND AND PROCLAIM/ We beg you to turn the Dharma wheel, and proclaim THE PROFOUND, FAR-REACHING SOUND/ You simply <u>must</u> proclaim the profound, far-reaching sound. Would you say it was far reaching, or not? Shakyamuni Buddha is telling us about the Buddha Great-Penetrating-Wisdom-Victory. Wouldn't you say his sound has reached far into the future?

Sutra: T. 24 b 9

Thereupon, the Thus-Come-One Great-Penetrating-Wisdom-Victory assented by his silence.

Outline:

N6. The Thus Come One assents by silence.

1246

Commentary:

THEREUPON, THE THUS-COME-ONE GREAT-PENETRATING-WISDOM-
VICTORY ASSENTED BY HIS SILENCE.   He had been asked to
speak the Dharma.   His silence indicated that he would do
so.

Sutra: T. 24 b 9
And so it was in all directions from the southwest to the lower direction.

Outline:

> M4. Including the
> other six directions.

Commentary:

AND SO IT WAS IN ALL DIRECTIONS FROM THE SOUTHWEST TO
THE LOWER DIRECTION.   This includes six directions not yet
mentioned: the southwest, west, northwest, north, northeast,
and the lower direction.   Since the process of seeing the
light, investigating it, following it and seeing the Buddha,
making offerings, and requesting the turning of the Dharma
wheel had been set forth for the gods in the east, southeast,
and south, that makes nine directions in all.   The last direction to be mentioned is the upper direction, which follows:

Sutra: T. 24 b 10
Then, five hundred myriads of millions

*of great Brahma Kings in the upper dir-
ections, seeing the palaces they rested in
shining with awesome brilliance as never
before, jumped for joy, thinking it rare
indeed.*

Outline:

M5. Above.

N1. Startled by
the portents.

Commentary:

THEN, FIVE HUNDRED MYRIADS OF MILLIONS OF BRAHMA KINGS
IN THE UPPER DIRECTIONS, SEEING THE PALACES THEY RESTED IN,
where they lived, SHINING WITH AWESOME BRILLIANCE AS NEVER
BEFORE... It was a state they had never experienced. They
were startled, amazed! Why? They had never seen such a
thing before. They JUMPED FOR JOY... They were so happy.
They were like children at their first puppet show; they
danced with glee and forgot all about who they were and
where they were and just jumped for joy, THINKING IT RARE
INDEED. They thought, "Since being born in heaven, we've
seen many fine light shows, but this is the best one we've
seen." And they were very happy.

Sutra: T. 24 b 12
They visited one another and discussed

*this matter, wondering,"why do our palaces
shine with this bright light?"*

*Then, in the assembly, a Brahma Heaven
King by the name of Shikhin, on behalf of
the Brahma hosts, spoke verses, saying,*

*Now, for what reason
Do our palaces shine
With such an awesome light
Adorned as never before?
Wondrous marks, such as these
We have never seen before
Has a great and virtuous god been born?
Has a Buddha appeared in the world?*

Outline:

> N2. Talking it
> over among them-
> selves.

Commentary:

THEY VISITED ONE ANOTHER AND DISCUSSED THIS MATTER.
Because the light was so unusual, they wanted to find out
where it was coming from.   WONDERING, "WHY DO OUR PALACES
SHINE WITH THIS BRIGHT LIGHT?"   They all got together for
a meeting, asking one another, "Does your palace shine with
that bright light, too?" "Yes! Does yours?" And they all

asked one another. Thinking it weird, they decided to go
find out.

THEN, IN THE ASSEMBLY, A BRAHMA HEAVEN KING BY THE NAME OF
SHIKHIN, ON BEHALF OF THE BRAHMA HOSTS, SPOKE VERSES, SAYING,

> " NOW, FOR WHAT REASON,
>
> DO OUR PALACES SHINE,
>
> WITH SUCH AN AWESOME LIGHT?
>
> ADORNED AS NEVER BEFORE,
>
> WONDROUS MARKS SUCH AS THESE,
>
> WE HAVE NEVER SEEN BEFORE.
>
> HAS A GREAT AND VIRTUOUS GOD BEEN BORN?
>
> OR HAS A BUDDHA APPEARED IN THE WORLD?

Sutra: T. 24 b 20

At that time, five hundred myriads of
millions of Brahma Heaven Kings, together
with their palaces, each with sacks filled
with heavenly flowers, went to the lower
direction to seek out this sign. They saw
the Thus-Come-One Great-Penetrating-
Wisdom-Victory seated on the lion throne
beneath the Bodhi tree in the Bodhimanda,
revered and circumambulated by gods,
dragon kings, gandharvas, kinnaras, mahoragas, and beings both human and non-

human. They saw, as well, the sixteen sons of the king requesting the Buddha to turn the Dharma wheel.

Outline:

N3. Following
the light, they
see the Buddha.

Commentary:

The Brahma Kings all got together in their palaces. Since their palaces can undergo limitless changes and transformations, "as you will," it is possible to use them as cars, planes, and even boats. The palaces are very much like our present-day cars, except that they are much bigger than cars. Each Brahma King brought his sack full of flowers. These sacks can hold Mount Sumeru! Mount Sumeru can fit in their sacks without even shrinking down in size. It's an inconceivable state. You can't figure it out with your ordinary mind. Scientists do their research and philosophers make their inquiries. They research and inquire coming and going, but they never get their questions all answered. Eventually they get old and their wits grow dull; their eyes go on strike, their ears refuse to help them out, and their teeth fall out. These signs are telling them that they should "know when to advance and when to retreat." They should know that their time to die is drawing

near, and that is why their six organs are all getting lazy.
They say, "We have helped you out for so many years. What
have you ever done for us, your eyes, ears, nose, tongue,
body, and mind, huh?"

"Well, nothing, I guess," you mutter.

"That's right. And now it's time to say fare-thee-well,
because we are splitting!" Then, you can't see, can't hear,
and your sense of smell starts failing. That reminds me, in
Paris there are people who make their living smelling per-
fumes. They can tell you exactly what fragrances are com-
bined to make any perfume. It may be made of hundreds of
different ingredients but they can name them all. However
they are prone to developing lung disease. Their lungs give
out, saying, "Knock it off, for heaven's sake. We can't
stand inhaling all that perfume." The tongue hangs in there,
however. No matter how old you are, you can still taste.
The tongue may have a sense of loyalty, but your teeth don't.
They run off.

"That's no problem," you say, "I can get false teeth."

You can, but they won't work as well.

I once had a conversation with an old man over eighty.
"Sir," I said, "you are advanced in years and have a great
deal of experience. No doubt you have seen people lose their
teeth."

"I certainly have," he replied.

"Well, have you ever run across anyone who had their
tongue fall out?"

"No, indeed I haven't," he said, "have you?"

"Of course I haven't!" I said. "If I had, I wouldn't asking you!"

"What are you asking me for?" he said.

"Since you don't understand, I will tell you. Why do people lose their teeth but never their tongue? It's because their teeth are too stiff and rigid. They insist on chewing on bones and other hard things. The tongue isn't so stiff. It's very pliable. The teeth know when to advance, but the tongue knows when to retreat. Consequently, one's tongue doesn't fall out, while one's teeth do. The teeth are like a knife made out of steel that is too rigid. When it hits a stone, it snaps in two. If the blade is just right it will give a bit when it hits the stone and therefore not break.

When the body gets old, it falls apart. Once the body starts falling apart, the mind starts going, and soon it's time to die. Nobody can avoid this.

The gods got in their palaces and went off with their sacks of flowers to seek out the light. They found the THUS COME ONE GREAT-PENETRATING-WISDOM-VICTORY, the Buddha of great spiritual penetrations, great wisdom, a great victor with great power in morality, samadhi, and wisdom. He was in the Bodhimanda beneath the Bodhi tree, the Tree of Enlightenment, seated on the Lion Throne.

He was being circumambulated by gods, dragon kings, gandharvas, kinnaras... Why do the kinnaras have just one

horn on their heads? Oxen have two horns, moose have horns
with lots of forks on the top, but kinnaras have only one
single horn atop their heads. Ku Hu said he saw a woman
who had two horns on top of her head. She looked just like
a woman except she had these horns. Hmm. How come oxen
have horns and dogs don't? What's the reason for this? If
you have been raised in a scientific society, you should
be aware of these things. The oxen didn't listen to what
their parents said. Whenever their parents said anything,
they would lose their heads, like an ox butting up against
something. "Hey! Shut up!" they said, striking out at
their parents, hitting them over the head with their
words. Kinnaras, now, they didn't strike out at both parents, only at their mother. They would listen to their
father, but not their mother. This was because they were
afraid they would get clobbered by their father! Since
they only struck out at one parent, they grew only one horn.
They wouldn't listen to their mother. They insisted on
listening to music, running off to the movies or going
dancing all the time. When they came back their mother
would entreat them: "Why don't you do a little work around
the house?" Hah! And then they'd blast her. "What? Me,
get a job? I've got a place to live and food to eat and
my allowance. What in the heck do I want with a job?" They
just did nothing but play and so they turned into musical
spirits, kinnaras with one horn on their head. Since they
like to play so much, they go play music for the Jade Em-

peror. The gandharvas love to smell incense, and when the Jade Emperor burns the incense, they run off to play music for him. They are incense addicts, sort of like present-day dope addicts. They get intoxicated on the incense and play music and jump around thinking it the greatest thing in the world.

Although asuras aren't mentioned outright in this list, they are implied. I have lectured on them many times before, but ultimately, I don't know if you would recognize one if you saw one. In case you wouldn't, I'll introduce you again. Have you ever seen people who are just downright hostile? who are always fighting? who carry guns and knives? They are asuras! There are household asuras, national asuras, and inter-personal asuras. In the home, they are people who just won't listen to each other. They prefer to fight and get all afflicted, thinking it more fun than entertaining guests. In fact, they would rather eat afflictions than food! The husband invites the wife to eat some afflictions, and the wife says, "Okay, I will return the invitation!" The two of them eat two helpings of afflictions but still aren't satisfied. They want to share it with their children. They have a meeting and invite the kids to join in. When the kids have had their fill of afflictions, they run outside and treat their friends to some afflictions, too. Their friends return home and invite their own parents to eat some afflictions. One may want to cut off afflictions, but it is not easy. They just

keep rolling along. That's the realm of asuras--ever-
widening circles of affliction. Afflictions in the home
all day long. They're filling and don't cost anything.
Better than bread and butter! Now do you understand? If
you have afflictions, you are an asura. If I have afflictions, I am an asura. If he has afflictions, he is an
asura. Afflictions just means getting angry, giving people
a bad time. It means thinking, "Everyone is bad, bad! I
am the only good person there is. Where can I go to get
away from these bad people?" You think about it all day
long, but you never come up with anything. Why not? Because you are afflicted. If you had no afflictions, you
would see everyone else as the Buddha. Just take me, for
example. I look upon all of you disobedient disciples with
such patience! I teach you to be filial to your parents,
but you aren't. I teach you not to get angry, and you insist on getting even angrier. I tell you not to have a
temper, and you say, "How can I do that? I was born with
this temper. It's my old friend. How can you expect me
to break off with my old friend?" You don't listen to me,
but I don't get angry. If you want to be asuras, it's up
to you. When you have been asuras long enough, you'll
turn into something else.

Garudas, too, are included in the eight-fold division. They are the great gold-winged P'eng bird. No one
has ever seen one. How big are they? Well, dragons are
several thousand feet long, and the P'eng birds eat them

like we eat noodles! They grab them by the legs, hold them
upside down, and gulp them down, one after another.

Now, if you want to see one, I'll let you see one. But you
must promise not to eat them. It's dangerous! If they see
a person, they will want to eat him. He will take you for
a lazy worm and swallow you in one gulp. How big is the
garuda? His wingspread is three hundred and sixty yojanas!
Pretty big! With one flap of his wings he fans the ocean
dry, and all the dragons in the sea are exposed. He gulps
them all down, as he considers dragons his optimal diet.

KINNARAS are partners with the GANDHARVAS. MAHORAGAS
are the big snakes. They aren't like the snakes that we
can see. They are so big that they wind around Mount Sumeru
three times. And just how big is Mount Sumeru? You don't
know? I don't know, either! If you opened your Heavenly
Eye, you would know, though.

AND BEINGS BOTH HUMAN AND NON-HUMAN. How do people
get to be people? If you are filial to your parents, you
can become a person. How does one get to be "non-human,"
that is, an animal, a hell-being, or a hungry ghost? By
not being filial to one's parents. People differ from animals, in that people know to be filial to their parents,
to repay their kindness, and to respond to their virtue.
Some animals know how to do this, too, but most of them
don't, because they don't have enough sense; they are too
stupid. Stupid people don't even know if you are being good
to them or not. Eventually, they become "non-human." REV-

ERENTLY CIRCUMAMBULATED -- the gods, dragons, and eight-fold division paid their respects to the Buddha Great-Penetrating-Wisdom-Victory.

...AND SAW THE SIXTEEN SONS OF THE KING REQUESTING THE BUDDHA TO TURN THE DHARMA WHEEL, to lecture on the Sutras, teach the Dharma, and transform living beings.

Sutra: T. 24b24

Then, the Brahma Heaven Kings bowed with their heads at the Buddha's feet, circumambulated him a hundred thousand times, and scattered heavenly flowers upon the Buddha. The flowers that they scattered were as high as Mount Sumeru, and they offered them as well to the Buddha's Bodhi tree. Having made offerings of flowers, they each presented their palace as an offering to the Buddha, saying, "We only pray that you will show us pity and benefit us by accepting and occupying these palaces." Then the Brahma Heaven Kings, before the Buddha, with one mind and a single voice, spoke these verses:

"It's good indeed to see the Buddhas,
Honored Sages who save the world

And who, from the prison of the triple
    realm
Can effect escape for living beings,
All-wise, revered by gods and humans,
Pitying the flocks of beings
Opening the door of sweet dew,
Vastly saving all beings.
Limitless aeons of yore
Have passed emptily, without a Buddha.
Before the World Honored One emerged,
The ten directions were ever in darkness,
The three evil paths increased,
And the asuras flourished,
While the hosts of gods diminished,
Most falling into evil paths at death.
They did not hear the Dharma from the
    Buddha,
But ever followed unwholesome paths.
Their bodily strength and wisdom,
Both decreased.
Because of offense karma
They lost joy and thoughts of joy.
They dwelt in dharmas of deviant views,
Not knowing the rules of goodness.

Failing to receive the Buddha's transforming,
They constantly fell into evil paths.
The Buddha acts as eyes for all the world,
And but once in a long while does appear.
Out of pity for living beings,
He manifests in the world,
Transcends it and realizes right enlight-
    enment.
We rejoice exceedingly;
We and all the other beings,
Are happy as never before,
And all of our palaces
Receive the light and are adorned.
We now offer them to the World Honored One.
May he pity us and accept them.
We vow that this merit and virtue
May extend to all living beings,
So that we and all beings
May together realize the Buddha Way.

Outline:

N4. Making offerings
to the three karmas.

Commentary:

THEN THE BRAHMA HEAVEN KINGS BOWED WITH THEIR HEADS
AT THE BUDDHA'S FEET, CIRCUMAMBULATED HIM A HUNDRED THOUSAND
TIMES, AND SCATTERED HEAVENLY FLOWERS UPON THE BUDDHA. THE
FLOWERS THAT THEY SCATTERED WERE AS HIGH AS MOUNT SUMERU,
AND THEY OFFERED THEM AS WELL TO THE BUDDHA'S BODHI TREE.
Although the flowers appeared to be piled as high as Mount
Sumeru, when you reached out to touch them, there was no-
thing there. You could see them, but you couldn't touch
them. It's sort of like watching a movie. You can watch
a movie with your eyes, but you can't shake hands with the
characters in it. It's a wonderful and inconceivable state.
When ordinary people look, however, there is nothing there.

HAVING MADE OFFERINGS OF FLOWERS, THEY EACH PRESENTED
THEIR PALACE AS AN OFFERING TO THE BUDDHA. The gods like
their palaces more than anything else in the world because
they are so comfortable. They sit in them and are perfectly
at ease, thinking of nothing at all. They don't think about
their father, and they don't think about their mothers,
their sisters, or brothers. All they think about are their
palaces, about how great they are, about how neat they are,
and about how comfortable they are in them--better than lying on the sofa! They are attached to them all day long,
and so, when they went looking for the light, they brought
them along. However, as soon as they saw the Buddha, they
got enlightened and wished to set their palaces aside.

SAYING, WE ONLY PRAY THAT YOU WILL SHOW US PITY AND

BENEFIT US BY ACCEPTING AND OCCUPYING THESE PALACES. Allow us to make this offering to the Buddha and thereby plant blessings before the Triple Jewel. Please accept these palaces and live in them. THEN, THE BRAHMA HEAVEN KINGS, the five hundred myriads of millions of them, BEFORE THE BUDDHA, WITH ONE MIND AND A SINGLE VOICE, SPOKE THESE VERSES. There were many of them, but they all had one, common mind and one single sound to praise the Buddha, Great-Penetrating-Wisdom-Victory Thus Come One.

Today I am very happy that my disciple's parents have come to listen to the lecture. I know that the first time his parents came here to visit, they were afraid that he was in great danger, and they came prepared to bargain with me. But now, this is their second visit, and they realize he is doing well; they are not afraid for him. What is more, they sat all through the lecture; that's quite inconceivable in itself! However, I believe that one's parents are always concerned for their children's welfare. Every move their children make is watched very carefully. It's like me. Wherever my disciples go, I find it very hard to put them down. I am always watching to see what they are up to. Have they broken any precepts? Have they been taken advantage of?

I want to announce something here at the Buddhist Lecture Hall. After this, whether you are a left-home person or a lay person, when your parents come here, they can do

as they wish. If they want to stand, they can stand. If
they want to sit down, they can sit down. If they want to
bow to the Buddha, they can, and if they don't want to,
they don't have to. One's brothers and sisters, however,
should follow along with our routine. Parents are older,
and we at the Buddhist Lecture Hall want to practice filial
behavior, and, therefore, we will not try to coerce them
into believing in Buddhism. But, you can lean on your
brothers and sisters a bit; it won't hurt. That's today's
announcement.

IT'S GOOD, INDEED, TO SEE THE BUDDHAS/ We feel really
good to see the Buddha. HONORED SAGES WHO SAVE THE WORLD/
We have met with a sage who can lead us from suffering to
bliss. AND WHO, FROM THE PRISON OF THE TRIPLE REALM/ from
the prison of the realm of desire, form, and formless CAN
EFFECT ESCAPE FOR LIVING BEINGS/ help them to leave suffering and attain bliss, and end birth and death.

ALL-WISE, REVERED BY GODS AND HUMANS/ PITYING THE
FLOCKS OF BEINGS/ He is greatly compassionate and merciful
towards all the different kinds of living beings. This
includes both sentient and insentient beings. It is said,
"The sentient and insentient alike perfect the wisdom of
all modes."

OPENING THE DOOR OF SWEET DEW/ "Sweet dew" is the
heavenly elixir of immortality. The Buddha speaks Dharma,
leading all living beings to end birth and death, and so
his speaking of Dharma is called the "Door of Sweet Dew."

VASTLY SAVING ALL BEINGS/ The Buddha doesn't just save one or two beings; he saves them all, without exception. LIMIT-LESS AEONS OF YORE/ HAVE PASSED EMPTILY, WITHOUT A BUDDHA/ Way back into the past, through limitless aeons, and upwards until now, the time has gone by emptily, for no Buddha has appeared. For some, it was one hundred and eighty aeons, and for some it was one hundred and thirty aeons. Here it is simply "limitless" aeons. Living beings' causes and effects all are different, and so they see different things.

BEFORE THE WORLD HONORED ONE EMERGED/ into the world, THE TEN DIRECTIONS WERE EVER IN DARKNESS/ lacking light, THE THREE EVIL PATHS INCREASED/ AND THE ASURAS FLOURISHED/ WHILE THE HOSTS OF GODS DIMINISHED/ MOST FALLING INTO EVIL PATHS AT DEATH/ The hells, the animal realm, and the path of ghosts gained in population. The asuras also grew in number. That makes Four Evil Destinies. WHILE THE HOST OF GODS DIMINISHED/ Because they did evil deeds, MOST FALLING INTO EVIL PATHS AT DEATH/ We should all think upon this; we are ever in danger of falling into the three evil paths. We should always strive to be careful and avoid them.

THEY DID NOT HEAR THE DHARMA FROM THE BUDDHA/ Since they didn't meet up with the Buddha, they had no way to hear the Dharma. Because they didn't hear the Dharma, they knew nothing about cultivation, BUT EVER FOLLOWED UNWHOLESOME PATHS/ Because they did evil deeds, they fell into the three evil paths. If one does good deeds, one rises to the heav-

ens or gains in good roots. They fell into the three evil
paths, because they lacked good roots.

THEIR BODILY STRENGTH AND WISDOM/ BOTH ALIKE DECREASED/
They lost their health and their wisdom. Day-by-day, they
decreased. BECAUSE OF OFFENCE-KARMA, THEY LOST JOY AND
THOUGHTS OF JOY/ They lost the happiness they were entitled
to. They even lost the concept of happiness altogether. THEY
DWELT IN DHARMAS OF DEVIANT VIEWS/ NOT KNOWING THE RULES
OF GOODNESS/ They knew nothing about the rules of goodness.
FAILING TO RECEIVE THE BUDDHA'S TRANFORMING/ Because
their karmic obstacles were so great, they were unable to
see the Buddha and unable to be taught by him. Therefore,
THEY CONSTANTLY FELL INTO EVIL PATHS/ Life after life, they
fell into the Three Evil Paths.

THE BUDDHA ACTS AS EYES FOR ALL THE WORLD/ AND BUT
ONCE IN A LONG WHILE DOES APPEAR/ The Buddha only appears
at long, long intervals. OUT OF PITY FOR LIVING BEINGS/
HE MANIFESTS IN THE WORLD/ TRANSCENDS IT, AND REALIZES
RIGHT ENLIGHTENMENT/ The supreme, right, equal and proper
enlightenment. WE REJOICE EXCEEDINGLY/ at our good fortune. WE AND ALL THE OTHER BEINGS/ ARE HAPPY AS NEVER BE-
FORE/ AND ALL OF OUR PALACES/ RECEIVING THE LIGHT, ARE
ADORNED/ All the palaces we brought with us are shining in
the Buddha's light. They are more beautiful than they have
ever been.

WE NOW OFFER THEM TO THE WORLD HONORED ONE/ MAY HE
PITY US AND ACCEPT THEM/ mercifully accept our offering.

WE VOW THAT THIS MERIT AND VIRTUE/ gained by making this offering to the Buddha MAY EXTEND TO ALL LIVING BE- INGS/ SO THAT WE AND ALL BEINGS/ MAY TOGETHER REALIZE THE BUDDHA WAY/ the Way of Buddhahood.

Sutra: T. 24b23

At that time, the five hundred myriads of millions of Brahma Heaven Gods, having praised the Buddha in verse, addressed the Buddha, saying, "We only pray that the world Honored One will turn the Dharma Wheel to bring tranquility and liberation to many beings." Then, the Brahma Heaven King spoke these verses of praise:

" World Honored One, turn the Dharma Wheel
Sound the sweet dew Dharma-drum,
To cross over tormented living beings,
Showing them Nirvana's path.
Pray, accept our request,
And, with the great and subtle sound,
Pity us, and set forth,
Dharma gathered through countless aeons.

Outline:

N5. Requesting the
turning of the Dharma
Wheel.

Commentary:

AT THAT TIME, THE FIVE HUNDRED MYRIADS OF MILLIONS
OF BRAHMA HEAVEN GODS --actually, there were not just five
hundred, but five thousand or more, myriads of millions
of gods from the ten directions-· HAVING PRAISED THE BUDDHA
IN VERSE, each assembly of gods from the ten directions
had spoken their verses, and then they ADDRESSED THE BUD-
DHA, SAYING, "WE ONLY PRAY THAT THE WORLD HONORED ONE WILL
TURN THE DHARMA WHEEL, speak the Dharma to teach and trans-
form living beings.   Before the Buddha speaks Dharma,
someone must request it.   ...TO BRING TRANQUILITY AND
LIBERATION TO MANY BEINGS," happiness and salvation.   THEN,
THE BRAHMA HEAVEN KING SPOKE THESE VERSES OF PRAISE:

"WORLD HONORED ONE, TURN THE DHARMA WHEEL/ We Brahma
Kings and all living beings wish that the Buddha would
turn the great Dharma wheel to teach us all.   SOUND THE
SWEET DEW DHARMA-DRUM/ so we can end birth and death with
the sweet dew of Dharma.   TO CROSS OVER TORMENTED LIVING
BEINGS/ all beings suffering the agonies of the Three Evil
Paths, SHOWING THEM NIRVANA'S PATH/ the pathway to non-
production and non-extinction.   Point it out clearly to
us, so we can cultivate it.   PRAY, ACCEPT OUR REQUEST/

to turn the Dharma Wheel, AND, WITH THE GREAT AND SUBTLE SOUND/ the inconceivable sound, speak Dharma for us. PITY US, AND SET FORTH/ Be compassionate to us, and speak DHARMA GATHERED THROUGH COUNTLESS AEONS/ gathered through successful cultivation throughout limitless aeons. Proclaim the wonderful Dharma for the sake of living beings.

The great Brahma Heaven Kings have requested the Buddha Great-Penetrating-Wisdom-Victory to turn the Dharma Wheel. Here in the Buddhist Lecture Hall we speak the Dharma and teach the Sutras, and that is also turning the Dharma Wheel. We lecture here every day. The Wheel turns from morning 'til night. The turners get very tired but they continue to turn the wheel. Not only does it turn here but it turns in Los Angeles as well. Next Friday we are going to Los Angeles to turn the Dharma Wheel there. Six people are going; they represent the six perfections: giving, morality, patience, vigor, concentration, and wisdom. Kuo Li and Kuo Shan have invited us to their parents home in Los Angeles to speak the Dharma. I hear a lot of people are coming to the Dharma Assembly. In the Buddhist Lecture Hall, we have turned the Dharma Wheel every day until we are very tired. Probably, in Los Angeles we will be even more worn out. We might not even get to sleep at night! Whoever is afraid of over-exertion should back out now, while there's still time. If you don't chicken out, that means you aren't afraid of fatigue. You're wearing your armor of vigor, working in the six periods of the day and night. You must act as a good model for the lay people in Los Angeles. Last time I went to Los Angeles with Kuo Li for a Ch'an Session, he planted a Bodhi seed there and later took refuge. Now he has invited us there to turn the Dharma Wheel. This is a case of cause and effect which is quite inconceivable. When I went last time, a lot of people wanted to take refuge, but the person I went with was a Chinese who was jealous of the Americans and didn't want them to take refuge with me. He put himself in their way. But the seed, once planted, will come up sooner or later; you can't obstruct it forever. When the time comes the Bodhi sprout will come up anyway, and no rocks can keep it down. It will sprout and grow and bear fruit naturally. If you aren't afraid of suffering, you'll be able to teach and transform a lot of people. If you're half asleep, people will think, "What is this cultivation? They are our guests, and they're sound asleep! As soon as I open my mouth to lecture, my five disciples fall asleep on cue: "Let's sleep. Let's not listen!" If you do that no one will give rise to faith. So I hope you will sleep a bit less. Each of the five of you should prepare one lecture for each day. You can speak to them in English. Prepare something you'd like to say for twenty minutes or so.

Last year, on the eighth day of the twelfth lunar month, some of you made vows. Kuo I and Kuo Hsiu wrote out their vows. Kuo Ning also made ten vows, one of which was to save the insane and to save demons. Whoever is insane now has a chance to be saved and the demons also have a chance. I'm sure that no one has ever made such "crazy" vows before. Kuo Ch'ien wrote his out and read them quite properly, but I never knew what they were because he didn't write them in Chinese for me. I got the general gist of them, and they were not bad. Someone later told me that they were very good. Whoever else would like to make vows can do so on the tenth. We will also transmit the Bodhisattva precepts on that day and the Three Refuges. Taking refuge, taking precepts, and making vows: faith, vows, and practice. The sooner you make vows, the better. The sooner you take refuge, the better. The sooner you leave home, the better. Kuo Ch'ien left home first. Kuo Hsiu is actually the oldest, but she left home last, so, as far as cultivation goes, she is the youngest. I hope she hurries up and gets enlightened so she can be an enlightened Bhikshuni. In all things, you should strive to go forward and never retreat. Go forward in taking refuge, making vows, and leaving home.

Sutra: T. 25 a 1

At that time, the Thus-Come-One Great-Penetrating-Wisdom-Victory, having received the request of the Brahma Heaven Kings of the ten directions, as well as the sixteen princes...

Outline:

> J2. Nearby cause.

>> K1. Turning the Dharma wheel
>> of the half word teaching.

>>> L1. Receiving the request.

Commentary:

AT THAT TIME, right after the great Brahma Kings from the ten directions had praised the Buddha, THE THUS-COME-ONE GREAT-PENETRATING-WISDOM-VICTORY, HAVING RECEIVED THE REQUEST OF THE BRAHMA HEAVEN KINGS OF THE TEN DIRECTIONS, AS WELL AS THE SIXTEEN PRINCES...

Sutra: T. 25 a 2

Thereupon, three times turned the Dharma wheel of twelve parts which cannot be turned by shramanas, Brahmans, gods, maras, Brahmas, or other beings of the world. He said, "This is suffering. This is the origination of suffering. This is the extinction of suffering. This is the way to the extinction of suffering...

Outline:

> L2. Turning proper.
>
> M1. The Four Truths.

Commentary:

There are three turnings of the Dharma Wheel of twelve parts, also called "the three turnings of the Four Truths": the Demonstation Turning, the Certification Turning, and the Exhortation Turning. Everyone should know them.

The Four Truths are suffering, origination, extinction, and the Path. What is suffering? Happiness is suffering. Whatever you like is suffering. You like to get angry? That's suffering! You like to sleep? That's suffering. The things you like bring you suffering.

Right after each Buddha becomes a Buddha, he preaches the Four Truths, and then the Twelve Conditioned Causes, and after that, the Six Perfections. That's the order in which he rolls the Wheel of Dharma.

The First of the Three Turnings of the Dharma Wheel of Twelve Parts is the Demonstration Turning:

1. This is suffering, it's nature is oppression. If you get angry, your temper oppresses you so that you are uncomfortable walking, standing, sitting, and even lying down.

2. This is origination, its nature is seduction. It beckons you. You respond to the stimulus. This refers to the accumulation of afflictions, one on top of another.

You didn't want to get angry, but some situation triggered
that response and you did. You were "seduced" into it.

3. This is extinction, its nature is that it can be
certified to.

4. This is the Path; its nature is that it can be cultivated.

That's the first turning. The second turning is
called the Exhortation Turning:

1. This is suffering, you should know it.

2. This is origination, you should cut it off.

3. This is extinction, you should certify to it.

4. This is the Path, you should cultivate it.

This means that you should not only know about the
Four Truths, but you should practice them: know suffering,
cut off origination, long for extinction, and cultivate the
Path.

Knowing suffering, you should put a stop to suffering.
If you want to stop suffering, first of all you must get
rid of affliction, that is, cut off origination. If you
have afflictions, you will suffer. Without afflictions,
there is no suffering. You must long for extinction and
cultivate the Way. In this, the second turning, then, you
are exhorted to do these things.

The third turning is the Certification Turning. The
first turning tells you about this Dharma-door. The second
turning exhorts you to cultivate. The third turning Certifies that the Buddha has perfected it.

1. This is suffering. I already know it. I don't need to know it further.

2. This is origination. I have already cut it off. I don't need to certify to it further.

3. This is extinction. I have already certified to it. I don't need to cerfity to it further.

4. This is the Path. I have already cultivated it. I don't need to cultivate it further.

WHICH CANNOT BE TURNED BY SHRAMANAS --those who diligently cultivate morality, samadhi, and wisdom and put to rest greed, hatred, and stupidity. Left-home people are all called Shramanas.

You say, "I know that as a Shramana it is my duty to cultivate morality, samadhi, and wisdom and put to rest greed, hatred, and stupidity. That is why, every day, I bow to the Buddha, recite Sutras, bow repentances, and bow to Sutras. I work real hard. Isn't that diligently cultivating morality, samadhi, and wisdom?"

That's right! It's pretty easy, too, except that you get a bit tired after a while. Working so hard, you get tired and start thinking about taking a rest.

It may be easy to cultivate diligently morality, samadhi, and wisdom, but is definitely not easy to put to rest greed, hatred, and stupidity. Greed: "Ahh...I'm not greedy for money. I don't climb on conditions." You may not be greedy for money, but sometimes you get greedy for sex. Or, if you aren't greedy for sex, you may get hung up on food!

Money is All-Powerful, you know. You can buy anything with
it.

"If you are going to die, you can't buy your life," you
say.

Sometimes you can! Let's say you have committed a
capital crime and have been sentenced to death. If you
offer the judge several million dollars, some judges might
take the money and let you go. See? They say that money
can get you through to the spirits.

"I don't care if it can. I'm not going to be greedy
for it," you reply.

Well, perhaps you aren't greedy for money, but you
may then be greedy for sex. "Sex" doesn't just mean sexual relations; it refers to craving for material beauty of
any sort--fine clothes, a trim figure, a new hat... It's
all an expression of the libido.

And then, of course, there's food. You may deny that
you are greedy for sex, but at lunch time you load up on
the most nutritious foods and then take your vitamins. This
is all greed, you know.

"Well what can I do?" you wonder.

When it comes to clothing, food, and shelter, you
should be like this:

> The eyes see forms outside,
>> but inside there is nothing.
> The ears hear mundane sound;
>> but the mind doesn't know.

When it comes to eating:

> You eat each day, but don't taste a grain
> of rice.

"Sure," you say, "I don't taste one grain of rice. I taste a lot of them. I'm not Shakyamuni Buddha, sitting in Snow Mountain eating one grain of wheat and one sesame seed a day, you know."

You certainly can count better than I can.

> All day, you wear your clothes,
> but you don't put on a single thread.

"Of course I don't just wear one thread!" you say in surprise. "I wear a whole bunch of threads!"

That's not what I mean. When I say "not a single thread," I mean not even one single thread.

"But you must be stretching the truth."

When I say, "You eat each day but don't taste a grain of rice; all day, you wear your clothes, but you don't wear a single thread," I mean that you aren't preoccupied with food and clothing. You are not expending a lot of energy on eating and wearing clothes. You "eat without eating," and "wear clothes without wearing them."

"Not bad," you say, "Then can I go out and kill a few people, 'killing without killing?' Can I 'steal without stealing?'"

If you have no mind, no thought, you are not committing

1276

an offense. But, if you have the thought, it's definitely
an offense. Here, it's not that you don't eat, you do; you
just aren't attached to eating. You wear clothes, but you
are not attached to wearing them. This is what The Vajra
Sutra means by, "Producing that thought which is nowhere
supported."

"Dharma Master," you say, "the more you try to explain
it, the more puzzling it seems to get."

Of course you don't understand it. If you understood
it, you would be lecturing the Sutras.

"But I do lecture the Sutras."

Maybe you do, but you still don't understand this principle. Wait until you understand it, and then you can explain it, too. In the Ch'an School, the principles taught
are directed at separating you from all attachments.

Shramanas destroy greed, hatred, and stupidity. Hatred
is not easy to overcome. You may make a vow not to get angry, to obey your teacher, and be filial, and then--who knows
where or why--suddenly, you get mad. Your temper pops out
like a mouse out of its mousehole. The mouse of your temper hides in its invisible hole and shows itself unexpectedly.
Stupidity. What's that? It's just doing dumb things, unin-
telligent things. You may clearly know that something is
wrong, not in accord with Dharma, but insist on doing it anyway. That's stupidity.

Shramanas diligently cultivate morality, samadhi, and
wisdom and put to rest greed, hatred, and stupidity.

BRAHMANS are an outside Way. They wear robes and do various things, but they don't cultivate according to Dharma. The word Brahma means "pure will," and they used to cultivate pure conduct. Now they don't even do that. They're all murky. With the passage of time, no matter what it is, there are bound to be false versions of it appearing. In China, the Taoists are the equivalent of Brahmans. In Taoism they talk about the three classes: the upper pure class, extreme pure ones, and the jade pure ones.

GODS. Those who cultivate the five precepts and the ten good deeds are born in the heavens and become gods. MARAS are demons. They kill living beings. The Buddha saves and the demons kill. BRAHMAS, OR OTHER BEINGS OF THE WORLD. The Buddha, and only the Buddha, can turn the Dharma Wheel of the Four Truths. Gods, demons, those of other religions--none of them can turn it.

HE SAID, "THIS IS SUFFERING. THIS IS THE ORIGINATION OF SUFFERING. THIS IS THE EXTINCTION OF SUFFERING. THIS IS THE WAY TO THE EXTINCTION OF SUFFERING," the Dharma-door of the Four Truths.

Sutra: T. 25 a 4

And he extensively set forth the Dharma of the twelve causes and conditions: ignorance conditions dispositions. Dispositions condition consciousness. Consciousness conditions name and form. Name and form condition the six sense organs. The six sense organs condition contact. Contact conditions feeling. Feeling conditions craving. Craving conditions grasping. Grasping conditions becoming. Becoming conditions birth. Birth conditions old age and death, worry, grief, suffering and distress. When ignorance is extinguished, dispositions are extinguished. When dispositions are extinguished, then consciousness is extinguished. When consciousness is extinguished, then name and form are extinguished. When name and form are extinguished, then the six sense organs are extinguished. When the six sense organs are extinguished, then contact is extinguished. When contact is extinguished, then feeling is extinguished. When feeling is extinguished then craving is extinguished. When craving is extinguished, then grasping is extinguished. When grasping is extinguished, then becoming is extinguished. When becoming is extinguished, then birth is extinguished. When birth is extinguished, then old age and death, worry, grief, suffering and distress are extinguished.

Outline:

> M2. The twelve
>
> causes and condi-
>
> tions.

Commentary:

HE EXTENSIVELY SET FORTH THE DHARMA OF THE TWELVE
CAUSES AND CONDITIONS. You have heard about them many
times before. The list here is given twice. In the first
list of twelve, they give rise to one another. This is
called "the door of production." In the second list of
twelve, they are extinguished one after another in turn,
and this is called "the door of returning to extinction."
This is the Dharma cultivated by the Conditioned Enlightened Ones. The Sound Hearers cultivate the Four Truths.
Right after the Buddha realized the Way, he first taught
the Four Truths and then the Twelve Causes and Conditions.

You say, "I have heard the Twelve Causes and Conditions
listed many times, and I don't understand them at all."

I present them to you so that you can become familiar
with them and cultivate according to them. To really understand them, however, you must first certify to the Fourth
Fruition of Arhatship. When you get enlightened, you'll understand them. Before you've been enlightened, you won't
be able to understand them. So, don't worry about it. Just
investigate it: ignorance conditions activity...and so on.
Keep looking into it until, suddenly, you'll understand.

Sutra: T. 25 a 12

When the Buddha spoke this Dharma, amidst the great assembly of gods and humans, six hundred myriads of millions of nayutas of human beings, because they did not grasp at any dharmas, had their minds liberated from all outflows. All attained profound and subtle Dhyana concentration, the Three Clarities, the Six Penetrations, and perfected the Eight Liberations. The second, third, and fourth times he set forth this Dharma, thousands of millions of nayutas of living beings, their numbers like the Ganges' sands, also because they did not grasp at any dharmas, had their minds liberated from outflows. From that time onwards, the assembly of Sound Hearers was unlimited, boundless, and unreckonable.

Outline:

> L3. Attaining the Way
> upon hearing the Dharma.

Commentary:

WHEN THE BUDDHA, Great-Penetrating-Wisdom-Victory, SPOKE THIS DHARMA, turning the Dharma Wheel of the Four

Truths and the Twelve Causes and Conditions, AMIDST THE GREAT ASSEMBLY OF GODS, the vast assembly of great Brahma Kings, who had requested the Buddha to speak the Dharma, AND HUMANS, the millions of living beings, SIX HUNDRED MYRIADS OF MILLIONS OF NAYUTAS OF HUMAN BEINGS, BECAUSE THEY DID NOT GRASP AT ANY DHARMAS..." What does that mean? If you don't grasp at any dharmas, how can you understand all dharmas? Grasp hear means "to take in," "to receive." It means that they did not accept any evil dharmas. It doesn't mean that they didn't accept any good dharmas. You may remember that Shariputra's uncle, in debating with the Buddha, took "non-accepting" as his viewpoint. Then the Buddha asked him, "If you take "non-accepting" as your viewpoint, do you "accept" that viewpoint, or not? Shariputra's uncle was stumped. How could he "not accept" his own viewpoint? That would mean he didn't even have a viewpoint. On the other hand, if he did accept it, then he was contradicting his first premise! He took it pretty hard, because before the debate he had made a bet with the Buddha, saying, "If I lose, I will cut off my head and give it to you. If you lose, Buddha, then you must return my nephew, Shariputra, to me, and I'll take him home." The Buddha defeated him with just one sentence, "Do you accept your viewpoint or not?" There was no way he could win! The Uncle had set up his argument, saying, "I won't accept anything you say, right or wrong, deviant or proper. I'll act like a deaf-mute. I won't even listen!" He thought

this was extremely clever   If he didn't listen
to anything the Buddha said   then he couldn't lose. The
Buddha simply replied, "That's fine with me, your viewpoint
of non-accepting. But, do you accept your viewpoint   or
not?"

   So, he lost. Scared stiff, he turned and ran. At
that time there were no cars or trains, and he didn't have
a horse. He just hoofed it down the road. He took the
"shoe-leather express." His legs were obedient. They
"accepted" his commands to run. He ran two or three miles,
until it occured to him, "I am a human being. I made an
agreement with the Buddha to cut off my head if I lost.
How can I run away like that? I'd better face up to things
and go back." Heroically, he ran back to the Buddha, saying, "Shakyamuni Buddha, I bow before you. I respect you
a great deal. I admit that I lost, and now I must ask you
to give me a knife."

   Shakyamuni Buddha said, "What do you want a knife for?
Are you planning on killing the Buddha?"

   "No!" he said. "I'm going to kill myself!"

   "What for?" asked the Buddha.

   "I agreed that if I lost, I would give you my head.
I lost, and, being a hero, I must keep my word."

   Shakyamuni Buddha said, "You are really stupid! You
have studied the Four Vedas and the other treatises for
eighteen years. How did you get so stupid?"

   "S-s-s-stupid?" he stammered.

"I don't accept your agreement, and I don't want you to cut off your head. I don't want your old head!"

The uncle thought, "The Buddha really is different from ordinary people. Great! Since I get to keep my head, I might as well give my whole body to the Buddha." Then he said, "Buddha, I'll do whatever you tell me to do!" and he left home. He had gone to get his nephew back from the Sangha, but he ended up leaving home himself. All because he took non-accepting as his viewpoint.

Here the text says, "BECAUSE THEY DID NOT GRASP AT ANY DHARMAS." This means that they did not accept any evil dharmas. It does not mean that they didn't accept any good dharmas. Because they did not accept any evil dharmas, then they HAD THEIR MINDS LIBERATED FROM ALL OUTFLOWS. What are outflows? If you want to know what outflows are, you should first find out what outflows are not, or, rather, what non-outflows are. I will give you an example: take a look at this teacup. Does it have any holes in it, any outflows? It has no outflows, of course, and so it can hold the tea. If it had outflows, it couldn't hold the tea. Would you say that our bodies had outflows or not? Hah! Our bodies are bottomless pits. You fill your body up today, and tomorrow it all runs out. Then you fill it up again, and the next day it all flows out again. Obviously one's excrement and urine are outflows. They flow out, and we have practically no control over it. Our bodies have nine orifices which constantly secrete impure sub-

stances: there's sand in the eyes, wax in the ears, snot
in the nose, saliva in the mouth, besides excrement and
urine. But, these are very common, ordinary outflows and
aren't that important. The greatest outflows are the ones
you aren't even aware of: greed, hatred, stupidity, pride,
and doubt. Greed is an endless outflow. The more you get,
the more you want. It's insatiable. If you obtain the
object of your greed, then you just want more. If you can't
get it, you get afflicted, your ignorance arises, and you
get stupid. Why do people do stupid things? Because of
hatred, which comes from greed. Greed, hatred, and stupid-
ity--these three poisons are everyone's outflows. If you
can be without greed, hatred, and stupidity, then you are
without outflows. If you have no afflictions and no ignorance, then you have no outflows. Those who have cultivated their dispositions will not get angry, even when
scolded. Even if you hit them, they won't get angry. It's
not that they are incapable of anger; they simply don't indulge themselves in it. Everybody has a temper. Even the
Bodhisattvas have tempers; the equal enlightenment Bodhisattvas still have one portion of temper, about as much as
a hair. If they break through this hair-like particle of
ignorance, then they can become Buddhas. But, because
they haven't broken through this ignorance, they haven't
become Buddhas.

We say, "break through" ignorance, but that has a neg-
ative connotation of destroying something. I lecture on

this principle a bit differently from others: I say you
don't have to break through it, you must transform it.
Change ignorance into wisdom. Ignorance is just your basic
stupidity. If you change it into wisdom, it disappears.
Prajna Wisdom is just that which is transformed out of ignorance. ALL OUTFLOWS, refer to greed, hatred, and stupidity, but you could expand this list to include the
eighty-four thousand outflows. In general, outflows are
just our afflictions. If you have one portion of affliction, you have one portion of outflows. If you have ten
portions of affliction, you have ten portions of outflows.
If you have a hundred, a thousand, or ten thousand portions
of afflictions, you have that many outflows. Therefore,
if you want to get rid of outflows, it's very simple: just
don't get angry. Get rid of afflictions.

"But, that's very simple," you say.

Simple it may be, but you can't do it! If you can do
it, it's easy. If you can't do it, it's very difficult.

Affliction is obviously no good; everyone knows this.
But everyone takes their afflictions as more important
than food. If they don't get afflicted for even the space
of a single day, they feel as if they hadn't eaten--they're
starving! Once they give rise to afflictions, then they
feel as if they had eaten their fill. They don't think of
anything at all--perfectly satisfied. They don't worry
about the house, they don't worry about their country, and
they quit concerning themselves with their own bodies. So,

I always say you take affliction as a meal and eat one
helping after another. At home, you eat home-type afflictions; at school, you eat school-type afflictions; in society, you eat society-type afflictions; in the country;
you eat national-afflictions; in the world, you eat international afflictions. Whatever you do you give rise to a
corresponding affliction. Whatever afflictions you have,
you can't put them down. You can't put them down; you can't
put them down. One year, you can't put them down; ten
years, you can't put them down; but after a hundred years,
you certainly must put them down. Hah! You'll have to
put down what you can't put down. You'll put down what
you can put down, and you'll also put down what you can't
put down. Hah! See? When it's all over, you'll still be
thinking, "I didn't get my fill of afflictions--yet." Wait
until next life and I'll eat some more. Then, in your
next life you will once again take afflictions as your
food and drink. That's outflows for you.

   ...HAD THEIR MINDS LIBERATED FROM ALL OUTFLOWS. The
text says that their minds were liberated, but it doesn't
say that their bodies were liberated. They still have bodies, so how could you say they had been liberated from them?
Their minds had been liberated. This means they had no
minds at all. But it wasn't like Pi-kan whose heart was
plucked out of his chest by the King of Chou. It means,
rather, that their minds were free of all affliction. The
absence of affliction is the attainment of liberation. Af-

ter all, what is liberation? It's just having no affliction.

When the Fourth Patriarch went to see the Third Patriarch, the Third Patriarch asked him, "What are you doing?"

The Fourth Patriarch answered, "I am seeking liberation.
Will you help me attain liberation?"

The Third Patriarch said, "Well, who has bound you up?"

As soon as the Fourth Patriarch heard this sentence, he
suddenly became enlightened. "Ah! I am free. No one is
tying me up. Why should I seek liberation?" Saying that
their minds had been liberated just means that they had no
more afflictions.

"I can't do it!" you say.

If you could, you would be liberated yourself! It's
just because you can't do it that you don't attain liberation. Your body can't be liberated, nor can your mind.

ALL ATTAINED PROFOUND AND SUBTLE DHYANA CONCENTRA-
TION. Is that something you attain? How do you get it?
The Heart Sutra says, "There is no wisdom and no gain."
Then, if there is wisdom, there is gain. Why does the
text say, they "gained" it?" Because they did have wisdom. With wisdom, they gained these qualities. Then how
did they get their wisdom? They got rid of their ignorance. Once rid of afflictions, they obtained wisdom.

You say, "Then I'll throw my ignorance away and get
some wisdom."

If you throw away your ignorance, you will throw away your wisdom as well. Then you won't have either one! Affliction itself is wisdom. If you don't know how to use it, it's affliction. If you can use it, it's wisdom. So we say,

Affliction itself is Bodhi,

Birth and death, Nirvana.

If, in the midst of affliction, you can wake up and turn that affliction into Bodhi, then, right in birth and death, you attain Nirvana. There is no Nirvana apart from birth and death, and there is no Bodhi apart from affliction. Before, when lecturing The Sixth Patriarch Sutra, I talked about Bodhidharma's two disciples, Fo-t'o and Yeshe. They said to the Venerable Yüan, "You see: The hand makes a fist and the fist makes a hand. Was that fast or not?"

The Venerable Yüan answered, "Very fast."

They said, "Affliction is Bodhi; birth and death are Nirvana--it's just that fast."

The Venerable Yüan was immediately enlightened. So, you shouldn't think that affliction is eighty-four thousand miles away from Bodhi. And don't think that birth and death are eighty-four thousand miles away from Nirvana. They are immediately interchangeable.

To attain the profound and subtle Dhyana concentration referred to in the text you must cut off affliction. Turn affliction into wisdom. It is profound as in The Heart Sutra, "practicing the profound Prajna-paramita." It is subtle as in the verse we say, "Supreme, profound, subtle, and wonderful Dharma..." Proficiency in Dhyana samadhi is not gained externally. It comes from the awakening of one's own self-nature. The self-nature takes itself across through a process of self-cultivation and self-understanding. You don't get it from outside. So don't seek it externally. It is the wind and light of your original home. Your original wisdom is within you. It is within your own self-nature. It is not external to it.

Dhyana is a Sanskrit word It means "stilling thought." It also means "cultivation of thought." Dhyana samadhi is the attainment of the advantages of "stilling thought." To gain skill in it you must actually practice it.

Attaining the profound and subtle Dhyana concentration, they perfected the THREE CLARITIES, the clarity of the Heavenly eye, the clarity of past lives, and the clarity of the extinction of outflows. The clarity of the heavenly eye is also called the penetration of the heavenly eye. It is called a "clarity" because with it one can see all marks. The clarity of past lives refers to knowing what went on in the past not only in one lifetime, but through many lives into the past. It means knowing in which life you were a Bodhisattva. "Ah! I have practiced the Bodhisattva Way in the past. In such and such a place I taught and transformed living beings. I did this in the past. I should continue to do so now." In the past you made a vow to teach living beings, and so now in the present you make that vow again. You sit there and see, "Oh, I left home during the time of Shakyamuni Buddha. Shariputra and I were brothers! My older brother leaves home in every life to be a Bhikshu and I should do the same. If he goes on ahead, I shouldn't fall behind." With the clarity of past lives you see, "In the past during the time of Shakyamuni Buddha, I went and bowed to him. At that time, I heard him speak the Sutras, and so now I am very intelligent and can understand all the Sutras as soon as I read them. In fact, if I don't understand something, I often have a dream and understand it through the dream. I dream,

> The phoenix hasn't come,
> And the river sends no map.
> I am finished.

That's something I said myself in the past!! Gee! I said those words in the past, and so, hearing them now I am deeply impressed."

"The phoenix hasn't come, and the river sends no map. I am finished." Those lines were spoken by Confucius, in The Analects. The phoenix appears when a wise man rules, as during the time of Emperor Shun, when these birds were often seen. During the time of Fu-hsi, a turtle rose out of the river with a chart on its back, giving him the idea for the eight trigrams of the I Ching. "But now," said

Confucius, "We no longer see such animals. Thus, I know it's all over. I'm not going to work anymore. I'm going to retire."

Or, they see, "In the past I was a thief. Now I am going to change and be good." Such are the benefits gained from knowing past lives. Others see, "Oh, how strange! In the past I have been a pig, a cat--everything! When I was a cat, I could climb trees. When I was a dog, I guarded the door. When I was a pig, I just loved to eat. Gosh! That's really weird. Like Chih-kung said, 'Ancient, ancient, strange, strange...'"

One disciple made a vow to become an animal to teach animals. At first, I was surprised that he wants to be an animal but, then I thought, "I think everyone at one time or another has been an animal." It's just that you've forgotten. Since you don't have the knowledge of past lives, you can't see it, and so you think you are so out-standing. Actually, we are all about the same. There's not much difference, really.

The clarity of extinction of outflows means that all faults and habits are gone, outflows are ended. The most important thing is to have samadhi. With samadhi you can arrive at the stage of no-outflows. As long as you have outflows, the cause of the hells remains, as well as the cause of the hungry ghosts, and the cause of the animals. If you have extinguished outflows, then you have closed the doors to the hells, to the animal realm, and to the realm

of the hungry ghosts. If you get rid of outflows, you're
safe. If you have any outflows at all, then they will always be cropping up all over the place. The three evil
paths will be waiting for you. The ghosts will be calling
for you to come to them, and the animals will be waving
frantically at you, saying, "Hey!! Come on over here!"

THE SIX PENETRATIONS, six spiritual penetrations: the
penetration of the Heavenly Eye, the Penetration of the
Heavenly Ear, the Penetration of Past Lives, the Penetration
of others' thought, the Penetration of the Extinction of
Outflows, the Penetration of the Complete Spirit. If you
attain these six penetrations, you can make infinite transformations, as you will.

The Heavenly Eye is difficult to obtain. Most people
would have to cultivate for five hundred great aeons in order to attain the six spiritual penetrations. If you have
planted many good roots in former lives, you may meet a Good
Knowing Advisor who will teach you a special Dharma-door.
Then you won't have to pass through five hundred great aeons
to attain the Penetrations. Of all the people who cultivate
the Way, why do so few obtain spiritual powers? It's because
the merit and virtue they have accumulated through cultivation does not exceed the amount of offense karma they have
created. So, not only do people not attain the six spiritual penetrations, but, even if they do obtain them, they
will lose them again. Everyone can count up their daily
score. During any given day, do you give rise to more pro-

per thoughts or to more deviant thoughts? Do you have
more false thinking or more thoughts of cultivation? You
should be able to figure it out for yourself. If you have
more false thinking than thoughts of proper cultivation,
then you have created more offense karma than merit and
virtue. If all day long you don't have any false thinking,
but just singlemindedly cultivate the Way, then you create
more merit and virtue than offense karma. It's a very important point. Some people cultivate and attain the five
eyes and six penetrations because they have little false
thinking and their thoughts of cultivation are firm and
single-minded. In the Buddhist Lecture Hall now, there are
many people who are just about to attain the Five Eyes.
Why? Because they cultivate the Thousand-Hands, Thousand-
Eyes Dharma of the Forty-two Hands. This Dharma will cause
you to increase your eyes and hands. If you feel that your
two eyes are not enough, you can grow some more. I'm not
joking! You can be meditating in one place, but you'll
know what's going on all around you outside.

"Isn't that just false thinking?" you say.

On the part of ordinary folk, it's not false thinking.
From the point of view of a Bodhisattva, yes, it's still
just false thinking. It depends on where you're at. What
for common people is false thinking, for ghosts is not.
Ghosts don't have "false" thinking, they have "rotten thinking." They just think about rotten things. When ordinary
people meditate and are able to go outside, that's not con-

sidered false thinking. But, for Arhats, it's false thinking because Arhats should always be in samadhi. When you
are in samadhi, you shouldn't be running outside to mind
other people's business. Arhats have some leftover habits,
habits going back many lifetimes and many aeons, which they
have not cut off. So, what for common people is false
thinking, for Arhats is not. What, for Arhats is not false
thinking, for Bodhisattvas is false thinking. You shouldn't
just think that false thinking is false thinking, and that's
it. There are many different varieties of false thinking.
What for Bodhisattvas would not be considered false thinking, would not be considered false thinking for a Buddha.
For example, I am teaching you to study the Buddhadharma,
and you, for your part, do not consider this false thinking.
But, from my point of view, it is false thinking. You guys
think, "Oh, probably I've got samadhi!" when in reality, it
is just still false thinking. It's very difficult to pin-
point these things exactly unless you really understand
what's going on.

    With the penetration of the Heavenly Eye, you can see
all the activities of the gods; you can also see what's going on among people. With the Heavenly Eye, however, you
can only see the gods moving around and stuff. You can't
hear what they are saying. If you have the Heavenly Ear you
can hear them talking. They might be saying, "Hey, what a
good kid, cultivating the Way. He can come up here to heav-
en with us pretty soon." You can hear them praising you,

"Oh, what a good boy. He has taken refuge with the Triple
Jewel. He practices Dhyana meditation and is fairly sincere.
He's so-and-so's disciple."

The penetration of Past Lives means that you can know
what people did in their former lives, what their former
names were, and what they did. You might realize, "Oh, I
met this person five hundred great aeons ago. Hmm...I think
he was my father then. And that person over there was my
mother five hundred great aeons ago. That one was my brother. That one was my sister." You'll know all those kinds of
things. How far you can see into the past--five hundred
years, five hundred centuries, five hundred aeons--depends
upon how much skill you have. Knowing that they were your
relatives, friends, siblings, or spouse, you can think of
some way to cross them over. "They were my family and
friends before, and so, no matter what, I am going to
think of a way to save them in this life, to help them get
enlightened."

The Penetration of Other's Thoughts is very strange.
Before someone says something, you know what they are
thinking. "Ah, that one is having such-and-such a false
thought. That one is thinking about her child, she really
can't put him down. That one is thinking about her mother
who is sick. She is very worried about her.˙ That one is
thinking about her younger sister, "I really want to cross
her over. Will she ever believe in the Buddha?" That one
wants to save her mother. That one wants to save his fa-

ther. See? Every living being has his own brand of false thinking. If you have this penetration, you can know what each one of them is thinking. But, you'd better be darn careful not to tell them that you know what they are thinking. If you do that, they won't be able to face you again. Why? Because you know their secrets. They will be afraid that you know all about them. Don't blurt out, "Hey, I know just what you're false thinking about. You're false thinking about New York." Don't tell them these wonderful things. You may know it, but just act like you don't know it. Pretend it isn't even happening. Then you can know their false thoughts from then on. Don't think that you can go telling people that you know what they are thinking.

The Penetration of the Extinction of Outflows means that you have gotten rid of all your faults and bad habits.

The Penetration of the Complete Spirit refers to having all kinds of power of magical transformation. You can be sitting in one place and at the same time go off to New York to play. You can go take a look at things in L.A. It won't even take you one second to make your return trip either. You can make a round trip faster than a rocket. But you have to gain this penetration first. If you don't have it, forget it.

This has been a discussion of the miraculous uses of the Six Spiritual Penetrations. Some people who cultivate really want to attain the Six Spiritual Penetrations. Before you have attained them, you may think that they are a lot of fun. Once you get them, however, you'll find that you run into a lot of trouble. Really! You'll get them and see, "Oh, the time has come for me to save that person. I should think of a way to save him." If you fail to save him, you've blown it. On the other hand, if you do save him, you have a lot of work on your hands. Getting the six spiritual powers means you're going to have a lot of things to take care of. You'll think, "I have so much to do, I don't even have time to meditate. Do this! Do that! My work is never done!" You may think you're busy now. Wait until you get the Six Penetrations. You'll be even busier.

"In that case, forget it," you say. "I don't want them."

That's perfectly all right. However, it's all a part of the Path of Cultivation, and eventually you must attain them in order to teach and transform living beings. Don't be afraid of too much work. The more work you do, the more merit and virtue you will have. If you just do a little work, you only gain a little merit. It's better to be busier than to take naps all the time. Those who cultivate must not be afraid of trouble; they should not be afraid of being too busy. Don't be afraid that living beings will be hard to save. The harder they are to save, the harder you must work to save them. If one doesn't listen to you, keep on instructing him until he does. Don't worry about the energy expended.

...AND PERFECTED THE EIGHT LIBERATIONS. In order to have the Eight Liberations, you must have samadhi power. Without samadhi power, you cannot be liberated. Unless you are liberated, you are tied up. Who ties you up? You tie yourself up!

The Eight Liberations are:

1. The liberation in which inside there is form; outward form is contemplated.

2. The liberation in which inside there is no form; outward form is contemplated

Inside, there is no emotional love, no material attachment, and no desire. Outwardly, however, form is still seen, but inside it is empty. When an external state arises and things are no longer empty, then you don't have this liberation. Perhaps ordinarily you haven't the slightest desire. You have no greed, no hate, no stupidity at all. That's called "inwardly there is no form." Inside you are very pure, clear, and lucid. But that is only when no external state exists to upset you. Once an external circumstance arises, your samadhi power is not yet perfect. When you see some external state, basically you shouldn't let it affect you. But, now you see a state, and you get all excited! Say, a lot of people show up and you fear trouble. You think immediately about running off to the mountains to cultivate alone, eat when you're hungry, sleep when you're tired, meditate when you feel like it, and recite the Sutras when you want to. You feel that would be much better than having to be with all these people. But such thoughts indicate that you are not truly liberated. You are simply attached, turned by states. If you are not turned by states, then as the saying goes,

> When you see affairs and are awake, you can
> transcend the world.
> If you see affairs and are confused, you fall
> beneath the wheel.

If you see something and you wake up, then you are liberated. You qualify for the second of the eight liberations: Inside there is no mark of form, and outward form is contemplated. You are not turned by external states.

3. The pure body of liberation certifies to the perfect dwelling. At this time, there is no inside or outside. This state is arrived at through the cultivation of Dhyana meditation at the level of the Fourth Dhyana.

4. The liberation of emptiness without limit. You realize that you cannot find the limit of space, that space is infinite. That is liberation.

5. The liberation of consciousness without limit. Consciousness is very subtle, and also boundless.

6. The liberation of nothing whatsoever.

7. The liberation of neither perception nor non-perception.

8. The liberation of the samadhi of the extinction of

feeling and thought.

The Storehouse Teaching is called the "Half-word Teaching." It was only "half." When you get to the Prajna Period, that is called clarifying the "Full-word Teaching" to the "Half-word Teaching."

THE SECOND, THIRD, AND FOURTH TIMES HE SET FORTH THIS DHARMA, THOUSANDS OF MYRIADS OF MILLIONS OF NAYUTAS OF LIVING BEINGS, THEIR NUMBERS LIKE THE GANGES SANDS, ALSO BECAUSE THEY DID NOT ACCEPT ANY DHARMAS, HAD THEIR MINDS LIBERATED FROM OUTFLOWS. FROM THAT TIME ONWARDS, THE ASSEMBLY OF SOUND HEARERS WAS UNLIMITED, BOUNDLESS, AND UNRECKONABLE.

Sutra: T. 25 a 18

At that time the sixteen princes all left home as virgin youths and became shramaneras. They all possessed sharp faculties and clear wisdom. They had already made offerings to hundreds of thousands of myriads of millions of Buddhas, purely cultivating Brahman conduct, seeking anuttarasamyaksambodhi.

Outline:

K2. Turning the Dharma wheel which gets rid of the "Half-word," and clarifies the "Full-word."

L1. All the kids leave home.

Commentary:

AT THAT TIME, THE SIXTEEN PRINCES ALL LEFT HOME AS VIRGIN YOUTHS. The Buddha's sixteen sons left the home life. This is called entering the Way as a chaste virgin. ...AND BECAME SHRAMANERAS. THEY ALL POSSESSED SHARP FACULTIES AND CLEAR WISDOM. "Sharp faculties" means that they had the six spiritual penetrations. Their eyes could talk! Their ears could hear!

"What do you mean, 'Their eyes could talk?' Mine certainly can't," you say.

Don't you know that sometimes people can communicate very clearly with just a glance? Isn't that like knowing other people's thoughts, like talking with your eyes?

Sometimes, too, the eyes can eat. When the food is brought out, you just see it, and you are full.

"Oh, that's just false thinking," you say.

You may think so, but when you attain that state, you really will be full right when you see the food. Your ears will be able to see, and your eyes will be able to hear.

AND CLEAR WISDOM, they were extremely intelligent.

THEY HAD ALREADY MADE OFFERINGS TO HUNDREDS OF THOUSANDS OF MYRIADS OF MILLIONS OF BUDDHAS, PURELY CULTIVATING BRAHMAN CONDUCT, SEEKING ANUTTARASAMYAKSAMBODHI.

Sutra: T. 25 a 21

They all spoke to the Buddha, saying, "World Honored One, all these limitless thousands of myriads of millions of greatly virtuous Sound Hearers already have reached accomplishment. World Honored One, you should, for our sakes, also, speak the Dharma of anuttarasamyaksambodhi. Having heard it, we will all cultivate and study it. World Honored One, we all aspire to the Thus Come One's knowledge and vision. As to the thoughts deep within our minds, the Buddha himself knows."

Outline:

L2. Request for Dharma.

Commentary:

The sixteen Shramaneras, the sons of the Buddha-Great-Penetrating-Wisdom-Victory, left home under the Buddha along with the five thousand myriads of millions of Brahma Kings and the hundreds of myriads of millions of gods and humans, and so on. THEY ALL SPOKE TO THE BUDDHA, SAYING, "WORLD HONORED ONE, ALL THESE LIMITLESS, THOUSANDS OF MYRIADS OF MILLIONS OF GREATLY VIRTUOUS SOUND HEARERS ALREADY HAVE REACHED ACCOMPLISHMENT. Now, in this Bodhimanda," said the sixteen princes, "there are limitless millions of greatly virtuous sound hearers. They have great virtue." What is great virtue? This means that in past lives they did many, many good deeds. They practiced much virtue, so they are called greatly virtuous ones. They are called Sound Hearers because they were enlightened to the Way when they heard the Buddha's voice preaching the Four Holy Truths. HAVE ALREADY REACHED ACCOMPLISHMENT. What have they accomplished? They have accomplished the fruition of being Sound Hearers. But now they have a certain doubt about whether or not they have truly attained Nirvana. They have accomplished the Sound Hearer's fruit, but have begun to give rise to the mind of the Great Vehicle.

"WORLD HONORED ONE, YOU SHOULD, FOR OUR SAKES, ALSO SPEAK THE DHARMA OF ANUTTARASAMYAKSAMBODHI. You who are honored both in and beyond the world, O Buddha, really should, for all of us living beings, teach the Dharma of the utmost right and perfect enlightenment. How do you cultivate this Dharma door which is given the name 'the fruition of Buddhahood?' It is the position of Buddhahood, but there must be some method by which this position is cultivated and attained. If there is no way to attain it, and you just say, 'anuttarasamyaksambodhi,' it doesn't mean a whole lot to us. How do you attain it? How do you arrive at that position? There's got to be a method. Someone must explain it to us. If no one explains it, we'll never understand it, and we'll never get there. The sixteen princes are seeking the Dharma

for the sake of the entire assembly of humans and gods. Basically, when they heard The Avatamsaka Sutra, the sixteen
princes already certified to the fruit and understood the
Dharma of anuttarasamyaksambodhi. Although they understood,
the others hadn't understood, and so they pretended that they
didn't understand, so they could request it for the sake of
other living beings. It's not the case that the sixteen
princes, the sixteen shramaneras, the sixteen Bodhisattvas,
didn't understand it. They did long ago.

Why do they ask the Buddha to speak this Dharma?
They want to seek the Dharma on behalf of all living beings.

Here, in the Buddhist Lecture Hall, everday someone
requests the Dharma. The ones who request the Dharma do
not necessarily not understand it. Some of them can explain it, too. In fact, some of them can explain it even
more wonderfully than I can. Why do they ask me to speak
it? Because, I speak Chinese. Most people don't understand Chinese, and so when they hear me speak, they think
it is really wonderful Dharma. Then it's translated by
these eloquent translators, and they translate it ten times
better than I speak it. That way, everyone gets real excited about listening to the Dharma. That's why they ask
me to speak Dharma every single day. Basically, I don't
teach you anything you don't already know. You can all
lecture better than I. But, since I am a foreigner, you
think a lot of me. There's a saying, "Monks from far away
can really recite the Sutras." The grass is always greener,

you know. I, being as shameless as I am, just go ahead and speak it, rapping away senselessly. I may rap senselessly, but you do not listen senselessly. In fact, by the time it is translated into English, it's not senseless at all. Before it's translated, it sounds all confused. "What's he saying, anyway? The people who know Chinese are all laughing, so it must be funny. Hmm..."

Anyway, the sixteen princes already understood the Dharma of Anuttarasamyaksambodhi, but still they asked the Buddha to preach it.

Let us take a look at what the word means:

Anuttara, means "unsurpassed" (無上 -wu shang). The Buddha's position is supreme, there is nothing higher. Samyaksam means "right, equal, and proper" (正等正 -cheng, teng, cheng). It is "right," in that it differs from the state of common folk who are unenlightened. Common folk are not enlightened. They don't wake up. If you tell them the truth about things, they think it's false. If you lie to them, they think you're telling them the truth. That's just the way they are. In fact, if you try to tell them the truth, they get afraid and refuse to listen. "I don't want to hear the truth! What would I do if I knew the truth?" They don't want the truth. They may stumble in here accidentally for a lecture, but they run out before it's finished. Why? Because they don't want the truth. I say that they don't want to hear the truth, but their rationale is that they don't want to hear what is false! Tak-

ing the true for the false, they wander around with their
false ideas all day long, thinking they are true. Since
they can't let go of the false, they can't understand the
Dharma, and they are not awake.

When the Arhats hear the Dharma, they wake up. "Yes,
that's the way it is, all right," they say. "It's really
true." Since they know it's true, they pursue that truth
in cultivation. One is taught to put everything down, and
they do just that! They see through it all. They break all
their attachments, put aside all their faults, and attain
freedom and mastery. That freedom and mastery is just awakening. They have attained right enlightenment, enlightenment to what is right. They have not enlightened to what is
wrong: i.e., they are not enlightened to the pleasures of
the senses, dancing, and so forth. They are enlightened to
what is right, "right enlightenment." They have not, however, attained equal enlightenment.

Equal enlightenment (等 -teng), means that they are
the same as the Buddha, more or less. The Bodhisattvas have
done this. Not only do they attain right enlightenment by
enlightening themselves, but they also enlighten others. "I
have come down this road, and I advise others to do likewise
if they wish to become Buddhas. Other paths are not as direct and never get you to the position of Buddhahood. One
might say, "All roads lead to Rome" (or to enlightement),
but some take longer than others. You could take one of
those roads and go down it all your life and never get to

Rome, see? Hah! This means that if you don't understand
the Buddhadharma, but you want to become a Buddha, you can
run around forever and never get there. Bodhisattvas can
enlighten themselves and instruct others. "Don't go down
that road. Take this one, come with me. You'll certainly
succeed." They help others to wake up so that they, too,
can attain the doctrine of enlightenment. "Oh? Not bad,
hey. Right on! I've been going down these crazy by-paths
for so many years, getting absolutely nowhere. Boy, I'm
glad I got directions from that Bodhisattva." Then, after
they go down the right road for awhile, they become Bodhisattvas themselves and can be equal with the Bodhisattvas.
They are equal with the Bodhisattvas, and, you might also
say, they are equal with the Buddhas, too. They have, for
all practical purposes, become Buddhas. There are two ways
to explain the word "equal." The ones who are already Bodhisattvas are said to be equal with the Buddhas, and the
ones who are becoming Bodhisattvas are equal with the Bodhisattvas.

You ask, "Well, are the ones who are becoming Bodhisattvas equal to the Buddhas?"

Oh, more or less. Why make an issue out of it? It's
really not that different. They may have right and equal
enlightenment, but their enlightenment is not "unsurpassed,"
like the Buddha's. The Bodhisattvas are still Bodhisattvas.
Their enlightenment is not supreme. The Buddha alone has
the unsurpassed enlightenment. The Buddha is, therefore,

called the Lord who is Unsurpassed, whereas the Bodhisattvas
are called Lords who are Surpassed, that is, surpassed by
the Buddha.

The sixteen princes, seeing the myriads of millions
become Arhats, realized they could not stay at the level of
Arhatship forever. They had to press on towards the Great
Vehicle, to study the Buddhadharma. And, so they asked the
Buddha to preach to them the Dharma of anuttarasamyaksam-
bodhi.

"HAVING HEARD IT, WE WILL ALL CULTIVATE AND STUDY
IT. Once you have spoken this Dharma for us, we aren't going to let it go in one ear and out the other, like a breeze
just blowing by. No way. We are all going to cultivate and
study it. Understanding the Dharma of utmost right, perfect
enlightenment, we will definitely practice in accord with
it. We will cultivate according to the method given us and
will not be lazy. Great-Penetrating-Wisdom-Victory Buddha,
don't worry about us! We will certainly be vigorous in our
cultivation. We certainly won't be lazy. We will forget
even about food, we'll be so vigorous. And we'll be so
happy, we'll forget about worrying. We will be so happy with
the Dharma that we'll forget all our troubles!

"WORLD HONORED ONE, WE ALL ASPIRE TO THE THUS COME ONE'S
KNOWLEDGE AND VISION. We here in the assembly have our
hearts set on attaining the knowledge and vision of the Buddha." What is the knowledge and vision of the Buddha? The
Dharma Flower Sutra talks about,

1. Opening the knowledge and vision of the Buddha.

2. Demonstrating the knowledge and vision of the Buddha.

3. Awakening to the knowledge and vision of the Buddha.

4. Entering into the knowledge and vision of the Buddha.

That is, opening, demonstrating, awakening, and entering the Buddha's knowledge and vision. The Buddha first spoke The Avatamsaka Sutra. The next teaching was the Agama teaching, the Storehouse Teaching. Next, he taught the Vaipulya Teaching, or pervasive teaching. The next teaching was the Prajna, or Separate Teaching, and the final teaching was the Lotus-Nirvana, the Perfect Teaching. Now, all living beings want to hear The Dharma Flower Sutra; they want to "get rid of the Half-word Teaching and be clear about the Full-Word Teaching." They don't want the Half-word Teaching. They want the Full-word Teaching. The Dharma Flower Sutra is the genuine, perfect, great teaching.

"AS TO THE THOUGHTS DEEP WITHIN OUR MINDS, THE BUDDHA HIMSELF DIRECTLY KNOWS." What's this? Are there deep and shallow thoughts in minds, or what? How deep are the deep ones? How shallow are the shallow ones? The deep thoughts are the ones that have been in there for a long, long time. They have thought for a long, long time about asking for this Dharma. Which Dharma? The Dharma of becoming a Buddha, the utmost right and perfect enlightenment. Ultimately, how does one cultivate this Dharma? You need compassion, kindness, sympathetic joy, and giving--the Four Unlimited Minds of the Buddha. You also need the uncondi-

tioned mind and the undefiled mind. An undefiled mind is
the most important. Take care not to have desire. If you
have desire, you are defiled. If you are defiled, you won't
obtain self-mastery.

One must also cultivate the Six Perfections and the
Ten Thousand Conducts, the Twelve Causal Links, and the Four
Truths--the Thirty-seven Wings of Enlightenment. These are
all Dharmas for becoming a Buddha. But there is a quicker
method, one which enables you to become a Buddha without
having to pass through the usual three great asankhyeya
aeons. What is it? The Shurangama Mantra, which we recite
every day. In the verse before the mantra, Ananda says,

> " The wonderfully deep Dharani, unmoving
>   honored one,
> The foremost Shurangama is seldom seen
>   in the world.
> It melts away my aeons worth of upside-down
>   thinking,
> So that I needn't pass through asankheya
>   aeons to attain the Dharma body.
> I wish now to obtain the fruit and become
>   an honored King,
> And return to save as many beings as there
>   are sand grains in the Ganges river. "

One can become a Buddha quickly, without passing through
those uncountable aeons. What for? So that one can re-

turn and save other living beings. That's what Ananda
said. If you can recite the Shurangama Mantra often, you
will certainly become a Buddha very quickly.

You say, "But the mantra is so long. It takes at
least twenty minutes to recite it once through."

Yes, twenty minutes is a long time to say a mantra.
But you take twenty minutes every day to eat lunch and you
don't feel that's such a long time, do you! You don't complain about how long it takes to eat lunch and try to cut
back on the time. Why complain about the mantra? Weird.
You sleep for hours at a time and never complain about getting too much sleep. Why do you not object to sleeping and
eating but object to saying the mantra? Hmm? I really
don't understand your attidue towards studying the Buddhadharma. You don't even have twenty minutes to spare. And
also, there's the Great Compassion Mantra and the Dharma of
the Forty-two Hands. Those are the most wonderful Dharmas
for becoming a Buddha. Those who cultivate these Dharmas
can attain the Five Eyes and the Six Spiritual Penetrations
very quickly. But you're afraid of all the trouble. You
think if you get those powers you'll have more work to do,
but by the time you've got them, it will be too late for re-
gret. Trouble or no trouble, you're going to have to take
the trouble, that's all.

"Well, I'd be better off to stay just like I am, then,"
you say.

Fine, if that's what you like. I never force people to do anything. It's up to each one of you to decide what you're going to do. Do what you like. Don't do what you don't want to do. But the methods for attaining the utmost right and perfect enlightenment are just the methods I have taught you. Today, someone said to me, "You have taught us so many Dharmas, I don't even know where to start cultivating. I don't know which ones to do. I'd like to concentrate on one single Dharma and succeed very quickly, but you've given us so many!"

Among the Dharmas I have taught you, there are those which one can specialize in exclusively. But it's like going to shcool. First you have to study all the materials assigned. Then when you take the test you may be asked one or two questions which are taken out of all the material. You must have studied all of it to be able to answer those few questions. And you can't take open-book tests in the Buddhadharma. Among all the Dharmas I have taught you, there is certainly one which will get you to Buddhahood, but you're going to have to learn them all to get there. It's for sure you'll make it. But if you start complaining about having too many Dharmas to study, well...why don't you complain about having to eat everyday? You have plenty of time to eat. You're not afraid of sleeping too much, either. Quite inconceivable. So, the text says, "WE ALL ASPIRE TO THE THUS COME ONE'S KNOWLEDGE AND VISION. AS TO THE THOUGHTS DEEP WITHIN OUR MINDS,

THE BUDDHA HIMSELF DIRECTLY KNOWS." The Buddha knows them
quite well. They are asking the Buddha to speak The Dharma
Flower Sutra. Their deepest thoughts, the Buddha knows.
The Buddha knew long ago that this was what they wanted,
but since they didn't request the Dharma, the Buddha didn't
speak it. Now they are requesting the Dharma, hoping that
he will compassionately receive their request, teach and
transform them. After the sixteen princes asked for the
Dharma, the Buddha was delighted, and he spoke the Dharma.

Sutra: T. 25 a 25

Then, the multitudes, led by the Wheel Turning Sage King, eighty thousand million of
them, upon seeing the sixteen princes leave
home, also sought to leave home, and the
king permitted them to do so.

Outline:

L3. The followers also

leave home.

Commentary:

THEN, THE MULTITUDES, LED BY THE WHEEL TURNING SAGE
KING, that is, the father of the Buddha, Great-Penetrating-
Wisdom-Victory, and grandfather of the sixteen princes...
He had millions of followers-- EIGHTY THOUSAND MILLIONS OF

THEM, UPON SEEING THE SIXTEEN PRINCES LEAVE HOME, renounce all their wealth and property, their wives and concubines, and become Bhikshus, they all decided to leave home along with them and become Bhikshus, AND THE KING PERMITTED THEM TO DO SO. He said, "Fine. Leave home. I'll help you out, in fact.   If any one of you need anything, I will give it to you." So all eighty thousand million of them suddenly had a patron, someone to support them. They weren't afraid, then, of starving, freezing, or dying of thirst or poverty, or anything else. They went right ahead and, with one heart, left home to cultivate the Way and become Bhikshus. In the future, they would all become Buddhas. A lot of them have already become Buddhas, and some are still cultivating and will do so in the future. Eighty thousand millions of them limitless aeons ago made vows to become Buddhas. Their patron was the Wheel Turning Sage King; he made it easy for them to cultivate the Way.

Sutra: T. 25 a 27

At that time, the Buddha, having received the request of the sixteen shramaneras, after twenty thousand aeons, then at last, amidst the four-fold assembly, spoke the Great Vehicle Sutra by the name of the Wonderful Dharma Lotus Flower, a dharma for instructing Bodhisattvas of whom the Buddha is *protective and mindful. After he spoke the Sutra, the sixteen shramaneras, for the sake of anuttarasamyaksambodhi, all received, upheld and recited it and keenly penetrated its meaning.*

Outline:

L4. The Buddha receives the request.

Commentary:

AT THAT TIME, THE BUDDHA, HAVING RECEIVED THE RE-
QUEST OF THE SIXTEEN SHRAMANERAS, AFTER TWENTY THOUSAND
AEONS, during which time he spoke the Vaipulya and Prajna
teachings, THEN, AT LAST, AMIDST THE FOUR FOLD ASSEMBLY,
--Upasakas, Upasikas, Bhikshus, and Bhikshunis--SPOKE THE
GREAT VEHICLE SUTRA BY THE NAME OF, THE WONDERFUL DHARMA
LOTUS FLOWER. This Sutra is A DHARMA FOR INSTRUCTING BOD-
HISATTVAS OF WHOM THE BUDDHA IS PROTECTIVE AND MINDFUL.
The Buddha watches over and protects those who recite The
Lotus Sutra.

AFTER HE SPOKE THE SUTRA, THE SIXTEEN SHRAMANERAS,
FOR THE SAKE OF ANUTTARASAMYAKSAMBODHI, the utmost right
and perfect enlightenment, the Buddha-fruit, ALL RECEIVED,
UPHELD, AND RECITED IT AND KEENLY PENETRATED ITS MEANING.
They recited it until they could recite from the beginning
to the end from memory! And they never forgot it; it stuck

1316

right in their eighth consciousnesses.

Sutra: T. 25b1

When the sutra was spoken, the sixteen Bodhisattva-shramaneras all received it with faith. Among the host of sound Hearers, too, there were those who had faith in it and understood it. The remaining thousands of myriads of millions of living beings, however, all gave rise to doubts.

Outline:

> L5. In the assembly, some understood and some did not.

Commentary:

WHEN THE SUTRA, The Dharma Flower Sutra, WAS SPOKEN, THE SIXTEEN BODHISATTVA-SHRAMANERAS, or, you could say "Shramanera Bodhisattvas." This means that they had received the ten Shramanera Precepts, but they had not yet received the two-hundred fifty Bhikshu Precepts. How could they become Bodhisattvas if they hadn't even taken the Bhikshu precepts? It was because the sixteen Shramaneras cultivated with great vigor. They were so vigorous, in fact, they didn't even have time to take the Bhikshu precepts!

Too busy! Busy doing what? Lecturing on the Sutras, turning the great Dharma wheel, and reciting the Lotus Sutra.
Basically, precepts are designed for those who need them,
that is, people who might not observe the precepts. If,
however, you are busy reciting The Lotus Sutra all day long,
you won't have time to break any precepts because you'll be
keeping strict control over the three karmic vehicles: body,
mouth, and mind. If you are reciting the Sutra with your
mouth, your mouth won't commit the four evils of the mouth:
lying, harsh speech, double-tongued speech, frivolous speech.
If you're kneeling there reciting it, you won't commit the
three evils of the body: killing, stealing, or sexual mis-
conduct. If you are keeping the meaning of the Sutra in
your mind, you won't be committing the three evils of the
mind: greed, hatred, and stupidity. That means you will be
pure in the three karmas. If you are pure in this way, taking or not taking the precepts doesn't matter. That's why
the sixteen Shramaneras were also Bodhisattvas.

What is more, these sixteen Shramaneras, althought they
were said to be shramaneras, were actually "people who had
come back again." This means that they were born into that
time and place in order to protect the Bodhimanda of Great-
Penetrating-Wisdom-Victory Buddha. In past lives they made
deliberate vows, saying, "When this person becomes a Buddha,
I am going to protect his Bodhimanda." This is like Kuo Hu,
who made a vow that when I become a Buddha, he will protect
my Bodhimanda. I haven't become a Buddha yet, and he is al-

ready protecting my Bodhimanda! He didn't even wait for me to become a Buddha. That's a real vow for you! Actually, when someone becomes a Buddha , he gains great spiritual powers and miraculous abilities, and it doesn't matter whether anyone protects his Bodhimanda or not. He can take care of himself. But, before one becomes a Buddha and gains spiritual powers, if you protect his Bodhimanda, then you are really protecting it. It's like, if there were a wealthy person who ate the world's finest food every single day, and you said, "Today I'm going to treat you to a fine lunch," he wouldn't necessarily be too excited, because he gets terrific food at home all the time. But, if you offered to take a poor person, someone who doesn't eat too well, out to lunch, he would really appreciate it. So, after this, if you make vows to protect my Dharma, don't wait until I become a Buddha to protect it. At that time, there will be a lot of Dharma protectors. When you really need Dharma protectors is before you have become a Buddha.

They ALL RECIVED IT WITH FAITH, accepted the wonderful Dharma spoken by the Buddha Great-Penetrating-Wisdom-Victory. AMONG THE HOST OF SOUND HEARERS, TOO, THERE WERE THOSE WHO HAD FAITH IN IT AND UNDERSTOOD IT. THE REMAINING THOUSANDS OF MYRIADS OF MILLIONS OF LIVING BEINGS, HOWEVER, ALL GAVE RISE TO DOUBTS. They had doubts about that wonderful Dharma.

You say, "The Buddha has great spiritual powers. For example, when the Sutra began five thousand people rose and walked out. Perhaps the Buddha moved them to another land altogether so that they wouldn't commit the offense of having doubts and perhaps slandering the Dharma." Just having doubts wouldn't mean that they would fall into lower realms, but if they went so far as to slander the Dharma, the Great Vehicle Scriptures, they would fall into the three evil paths. So, when Shakyamuni Buddha spoke The Dharma Flower Sutra, he forced the five thousand arrogant Bhikshus to leave. When the Buddha Great-Penetrating-Wisdom-Victory spoke the Dharma, thousands of myriads of millions of beings gave rise to doubts, so why didn't he have them removed to other lands to avoid their doubts? He didn't do this because he knew that, although they may have given rise to doubts, they would not slander the Dharma; so he didn't need to have them relocated.

Sutra: T. 25 b4
The Buddha spoke this sutra for eighty thousand aeons without cessation.

Outline:

L6. Period of time.

Commentary:

THE BUDDHA SPOKE THIS SUTRA FOR EIGHTY THOUSAND AEONS WITHOUT CESSATION; he spoke without stopping, without interruption. That's a long time. Shakyamuni Buddha spoke

The Dharma Flower Sutra in just eight years. Why did one
Buddha take so long and the other take such a short time?
Discriminations of short and long periods of time are done
by living beings. Really, there is no such thing as "long
and short" periods of time. "Long and short" are created
by mental discriminations. The Buddha Great-Penetrating-
Wisdom-Victory spoke The Dharma Flower Sutra, the real
mark Dharma-door, for eighty thousand aeons and Shakyamuni Buddha spoke this real mark Dharma-door for only
eight years, but there's no problem with the difference
in time. The Buddha spoke for eighty-thousand aeons without cessation. He didn't rest at all. He didn't ever
take a break. He spoke the Sutra every single day. Every
single day he spoke the Great Vehicle's real mark Dharma.
You shouldn't think it unusual that we have lectures here
in the Buddhist Lecture Hall every day. The Buddhas always lecture every day. Since we are the Buddha's disciples, we should investigate the Sutra every day, too. And
we shouldn't take a rest.

Sutra: T. 25b4
   When he had finished speaking the sutra, he
entered a quiet room where he remained in
Dhyana Samadhi for eighty-four thousand
aeons.

Outline:

> L7. After speaking the
> Sutra, he enters samadhi.

Commentary:

WHEN HE HAD FINISHED SPEAKING THE SUTRA, when he was done, HE ENTERED A QUIET ROOM, his meditation room, WHERE HE REMAINED IN DHYANA SAMADHI FOR EIGHTY-FOUR THOUSAND AEONS. When the Buddha was in samadhi, was no one lecturing on the Sutra?

Sutra: T. 25 b 5

Then the sixteen Bodhisattva shramaneras, knowing that the Buddha had entered his room and was silently absorbed in Dhyana Samadhi, each ascended the Dharma seat. For a period of eighty-four thousand aeons, for the sake of the four-fold assembly, they spoke the <u>Wonderful Dharma Flower Sutra</u> extensively and in detail. Each one of them crossed over six hundred myriads of millions of nayutas of Ganges' sands of living beings, instructing them with the teaching, benefitting them, making them rejoice and causing them to bring forth the thought of anuttarasamyaksambodhi.

Outline:

Commentary:

THEN THE SIXTEEN BODHISATTVA SHARAMANERAS, duirng the time the Buddha was in samadhi, KNOWING THAT THE BUD-DHA HAD ENTERED HIS ROOM AND WAS SILENTLY ABSORBED IN DHYANA SAMADHI... He was "thus, thus, unmoving, clear, lucid, and constantly bright" there in samadhi. They decided to keep on propagating the Dharma, and so EACH AS-CENDED THE DHARMA SEAT. Someone is wondering, "Did they all get up on the same seat, or what?" No! They took turns lecturing. And some went off into different directions--north, east, south, and west. Don't get to thinking that they all climbed up on the one Dharma seat. That would be silly.

'FOR A PERIOD OF EIGHTY-FOUR THOUSAND AEONS, FOR THE SAKE OF THE FOUR FOLD ASSEMBLY, THEY SPOKE THE WONDERFUL DHARMA FLOWER SUTRA EXTENSIVELY, broadly, AND IN DETAIL, they expounded upon the doctrine. EACH ONE OF THEM CROSSED

OVER SIX HUMDRED MYRIADS OF MILLIONS OF NAYUTAS OF GANGES SANDS OF LIVING BEINGS, INSTRUCTING THEM WITH THE TEACHING, BENEFITTING THEM, MAKING THEM REJOICE, AND CAUSING THEM TO BRING FORTH THE THOUGHT OF ANUTTARASAMYAKSAMBODHI.   All those living beings together produced the mind to seek the utmost right and perfect enlightenment.

Sutra: T. 25 b 10

After eighty-four thousand aeons had passed, the Buddha, Great-Penetrating-Wisdom-Victory arose from Samadhi, approached the Dharma throne and serenely sat down upon it. He addressed the great assembly, saying; "These sixteen Bodhisattva-shramaneras are very rare. All their faculties are keen and their wisdom is clear. They have in the past already made offerings to limitless thousands of myriads of millions of Buddhas. In the presence of those Buddhas, they constantly cultivated Brahman conduct, accepting and upholding the Buddha's wisdom, instructing living beings and causing them to enter into it.

Outline:

L2. The Buddha arises
and praises them.

M1. Praise.

Commentary:

The Buddha had been in his quiet room in samadhi, and then AFTER EIGHTY-FOUR THOUSAND AEONS HAD PASSED, THE BUDDHA. GREAT-PENETRATING-WISDOM-VICTORY AROSE FROM SAMADHI, APPROACHED THE DHARMA THRONE, he went to his Dharma seat, AND SERENLY SAT DOWN UPON IT. HE ADDRESSED THE GREAT ASSEMBLY, all present in the Bodhimanda, SAYING, "THESE SIXTEEN BODHISATTVA-SHRAMANERAS ARE VERY RARE. ALL THEIR FACULTIES ARE KEEN AND THEIR WISDOM IS CLEAR." "Keen faculties" means that they could use their six sense organs interchangeably. Their Prajna wisdom manifested, so that they clearly understood all Dharmas. Why did they clearly understand all dharmas? THEY HAVE IN THE PAST ALREADY MADE OFFERINGS TO LIMITLESS THOUSANDS OF MYRIADS OF MILLIONS OF BUDDHAS. IN THE PRESENCE OF THOSE BUDDHAS, THEY CONSTANTLY CULTIVATED BRAHMAN CONDUCT, they kept the precepts purely, ACCEPTING AND UPHOLDING THE BUDDHA'S WISDOM. They always studied the wisdom of the Buddha, INSTRUCTING LIVING BEINGS AND CAUSING THEM TO ENTER INTO IT, enter into the Buddha's wisdom.

Sutra: T. 25 b 15

"You should all make a point of drawing near to and making offerings to them. Why? Those Sound Hearers, Pratyeka Buddhas, or Bodhisattvas who can have faith in the Dharma of the Sutra spoken by these sixteen Bodhisattvas, accept and uphold it without defaming it, will all attain anuttarasamyaksambodhi, that is, the wisdom of the Thus Come One.'

Outline:

M2. Exhortation.

Commentary:

" YOU SHOULD ALL MAKE A POINT..." "Making a point" means to be quick about it. " ...DRAWING NEAR TO AND MAK-ING OFFERINGS TO THEM." Draw near to them, do not leave them, and make offerings to them. Make a point of doing it, time and again. " WHY? Why do I say this? THOSE SOUND HEARERS, PRATYEKA BUDDHAS OR BODHISATTVAS WHO CAN HAVE FAITH IN THE DHARMA OF THE SUTRA SPOKEN BY THESE SIXTEEN BODHISATTVAS, deeply believing it, without any doubts, AC-CEPT AND UPHOLD IT, not forgetting it, and WITHOUT ·DEFAMING IT, they WILL ALL ATTAIN ANUTTARASAMYAKSAMBODHI, the Sound Hearers, Pratyeka Buddhas, Bodhisattvas, or just living be-

1326

ings in general, they will all attain supreme enlightenment,
THAT IS, THE WISDOM OF THE THUS COME ONE. "

Sutra: T. 25 b 18

The Buddha told the bhikshus,"These sixteen Bodhisattvas always delight in speaking the Wonderful Dharma Lotus Flower
Sutra. Each Bodhisattva has transformed
six hundred myriads of millions of nayutas
of Ganges' sands of living beings who, life
after life were born together with the Bodhisattvas and heard the Dharma from them,
fully believing and understanding it. For
this reason, they have met up with forty
thousand millions of Buddhas, World Honored
Ones and to this moment have not stopped
doing so.

Outline:

> K2. Still meeting Buddhas in
> the interim.

Commentary:

THE BUDDHA TOLD THE BHIKSHUS, "THESE SIXTEEN BODHISAT-
TVAS ALWAYS DELIGHT IN SPEAKING THE WONDERFUL DHARMA LOTUS
FLOWER SUTRA, the thing they like to do best is to speak

this Sutra. EACH BODHISATTVA HAS TRANSFORMED SIX HUNDRED MYRIADS OF MILLIONS OF NAYUTAS OF GANGES SANDS OF LIVING BEINGS WHO, LIFE AFTER LIFE, WERE BORN TOGETHER WITH THE BODHISATTVAS...'" Each of the sixteen Bodhisattvas has transformed and taught millions of living beings, WHO, LIFE AFTER LIFE, WERE BORN TOGETHER WITH THE BODHISATTVAS. The beings taught and transformed by the sixteen shramaneras made vows in every life to be born together with these sixteen. HEAR-THE DHARMA FROM THEM, hearing the sixteen shramaneras speak the Dharma, FULLY BELIEVING AND UNDERSTANDING IT. They understood it and had no doubts. FOR THIS REASON, THEY HAVE MET UP WITH FORTY THOUSAND MILLIONS OF BUDDHAS, WORLD HONORED ONES, AND TO THIS MOMENT, HAVE NOT STOPPED DOING SO. "

Sutra: T. 25b23

Bhikshus, I will tell you, those disciples of the Buddha, the sixteen shramaneras, have all now attained anuttarasamyaksambodhi, and in the lands of the ten directions, are presently speaking the Dharma. They have as their retinues limitless hundreds of thousands of millions of Bodhisattvas and Sound Hearers. Two have become Buddhas in the East: One is named Akshobhya, in the Land of Happiness. The other is named Sumeru Peak. Two have become Buddhas in the Southeast: one is named

Lion Sound. The other is named Lion Sign. Two
have become Buddhas in the South: one is
named Space Dweller. The other is named
Eternal Extinction. Two have become Buddhas
in the Southwest: One is named Royal Sign.
The other is named Brahma Sign. Two
have become Buddhas in the West: One is
named Amitayus. The other is named
Savior of all Worlds from Suffering and
Anguish. Two have become Buddhas in
the Northwest. One is named Tamalapa-
trachandana Fragrance and Spiritual
Penetrations. The other is named Sumeru Sign.
Two have become Buddhas in the North. One
is named Cloud Self-Mastery. The other is
named King of Cloud Self-Mastery. In the
Northeast there is a Buddha by the name
of Destroyer of All Worldly Fear. The other
Buddha, the Sixteenth, is myself, Shakyamuni Buddha, here in the Saha World,
where I have realized anuttarasamyaksambodhi.

Outline:

K3. Showing how Dharma Flower
     is still spoken to the pres-
     ent.

    L1. Assembly present and
          past.

        M1. Teachers present
               and past.

Commentary:

Shakyamuni Buddha says, "BHIKSHUS, all of you, those who have left home and those at home, as well, I WILL TELL YOU, THOSE DISCIPLES OF THE BUDDHA, the Buddha, Great-Penetrating-Wisdom-Victory, THE SIXTEEN SHRAMANERAS, the sixteen little novices, big novices, older novices, sixteen in all..." Now, after you have left home for a long while, you can be called an "old novice." If you have left home for fairly long, then you're called a "big novice." If you've just left home, then you're called a "little novice." These were probably "older novices," because they had left home for a long time. Anyway, they HAVE ALL NOW ATTAINED ANUTTARASAMYAKSAMBODHI, enlightenment, AND, IN THE LANDS OF THE TEN DIRECTIONS, ARE PRESENTLY SPEAKING THE DHARMA, right now they are speaking Dharma. THEY HAVE AS THEIR RETINUES LIMITLESS HUNDREDS OF THOUSANDS OF MILLIONS OF BODHISATTVAS AND SOUND HEARERS. The Buddha's family is composed of Bodhisattvas and Sound Hearer Disci-

ples. They are like his children, his family. Since we
are now studying the Buddhadharma, we, too, are like the
Buddha's sons and daughters, his disciples. So, you must
be a filial child. We are all part of the Buddha's retinue.

TWO HAVE BECOME BUDDHAS IN THE EAST: ONE IS NAMED
AKSHOBHYA. "Akshobhya" is Sanskrit and means "Unmoving
Honored One." This is Medicine Master Crystal-Light-Thus-
Come-One. In our Buddha House we have the three Buddhas,
in the Center is Shakyamuni. On his left is Medicine Master Buddha, holding the pagoda, and on the right is Amitabha Buddha, holding the Lotus Throne. So, you remember
this, because when Americans see the Buddha images, they
always ask, "Who's that?" They want an introduction. So
Everyone should know who they are, so when they are asked,
they don't have to say, "I don't know," leaving people
thinking, "God, they live here, studying the Buddhadharma
every day, and they don't even know who these Buddhas
are!" That's pretty embarrasing. Not only for your disciples, but for the teacher, too. "What are they learning from that Teacher, anyway? They don't even know what
those Buddha's names are!" If new-comers want to know
who the Buddhas are, you who are here all the time should
pay attention to this detail. So, now I have introduced
you to them.

So, the Unmoving Honored One, Akshobhya, is the Buddha in the east. IN THE LAND OF HAPPINESS, that is, the

Eastern Pure Crystal World. THE OTHER IS NAMED SUMERU
PEAK; the second shramanera became a Buddha in the east,
by the name of Sumeru Peak; he is Akshobhya's neighbor to
the east.

TWO HAVE BECOME BUDDHAS IN THE SOUTHEAST: ONE IS
NAMED LION SOUND." He is called Lion Sound because when
the Buddha speaks Dharma it's like the roar of a lion,
awesome and fierce. THE OTHER IS NAMED LION SIGN.

TWO HAVE BECOME BUDDHAS IN THE SOUTH: ONE IS NAMED
SPACE-DWELLER. This doesn't mean that he lives in empty
space, just hanging there, for heaven's sake. THE OTHER
IS NAMED ETERNAL EXTINCTION; he is always extinguishing
the offense karma of living beings.

TWO HAVE BECOME BUDDHAS IN THE SOUTHWEST: ONE IS
NAMED ROYAL SIGN. He has the signs and characteristics
of royalty, like the god Shakra. THE OTHER IS NAMED
BRAHMA SIGN. In the causal ground, he always cutlivated
Brahman conduct, and so his marks are very pure.

TWO HAVE BECOME BUDDHAS IN THE WEST: ONE IS NAMED
AMITAYUS, also known as Amitabha. Amitayus means limitless life. Amitabha, his other name, means limitless
light. Here it is laid out very clearly that Amitabha was
originally one of the sixteen royal sons of the Buddha
Great-Penetrating-Wisdom-Victory. This Buddha's life is
limitless and his blessings and virtues are limitless. He
has limitless light, as the light of his wisdom is limitless. "Limitless life" refers to his blessedness, and

"limitless life" refers to his wisdom.

THE OTHER IS NAMED SAVIOR OF ALL WORLDS FROM SUFFERING AND ANGUISH. The other shramanera became a Buddha by this name.

TWO HAVE BECOME BUDDHAS IN THE NORTHWEST: ONE IS NAMED TAMALAPATRA-CHANDANA. Tamalapatra-chandana is, obviously, Sanskrit. Tamalapatra is interpreted as meaning, "worthy whose nature is without defilement." This means that his self-nature is free of dust and filth. He is a worthy sage. Chandana is a kind of incense. THE OTHER IS NAMED SUMERU SIGN.

TWO HAVE BECOME BUDDHAS IN THE NORTH: ONE IS NAMED CLOUD SELF-MASTERY; he can travel at will through the clouds. THE OTHER IS NAMED KING OF CLOUD SELF-MASTERY.

IN THE NORTHEAST THERE IS A BUDDHA BY THE NAME OF DESTROYER OF ALL WORLDLY FEAR. He can break through all the fearful situations. THE SIXTEENTH IS MYSELF, SHAKYAMUNI, which means "humane and silent," BUDDHA, HERE IN THE SAHA WORLD, WHERE I HAVE REALIZED ANUTTARASAMYAKSAMBODHI, the Buddha-fruit.

Sutra: T. 25c7

Bhikshus, we, as shramaneras each taught and transformed limitless hundreds of thousands of myriads of millions of Ganges' sands of living beings, who,

hearing the Dharma from us, were set towards anuttarasamyaksambodhi.

Outline:

> M2. The disciples of
> past and present.
>> N1. Great affini-
>> ties established
>> in the past.

Commentary:

"BHIKSHUS," Shakyamuni Buddha continues speaking to the Bhikshus, "WE, AS SHRAMANERAS, novices, EACH TAUGHT AND TRANSFORMED LIMITLESS HUNDREDS OF THOUSANDS OF MYRIADS OF MILLIONS OF GANGES' SANDS OF LIVING BEINGS, WHO...each one of us taught quite a large number of living beings." Here we are, Bhikshus, and we haven't taught or transformed a single living being. Shame on us! "HEARING THE DHARMA FROM US, studying the Buddhadharma under our tutelage, they WER SET TOWARDS ANUTTARASAMYAKSAMBODHI." Why did they study the Dharma? Because they wanted enlightenment. This shows that when they first heard the Dharma, they decided they wanted to attain perfect enlightenment. Each made progress towards it at his own rate of speed, but from here on out it was simply a matter of time until they achieved their goal.

1334

Sutra: T. 25c9

Of these living beings, there are those who dwell at the level of Sound Hearers. I constantly instruct and transform them in anuttarasamyaksambodhi. All these people will, by means of this Dharma, gradually enter the Buddha Path. Why? The Thus Come One's wisdom is hard to believe and hard to understand.

Outline:

> N2. Clearing up
> doubts of present
> Sound Hearers.

Commentary:

"OF THESE LIVING BEINGS, THERE ARE THOSE WHO already DWELL AT THE LEVEL OF SOUND HEARERS. I CONSTANTLY INSTRUCT AND TRANSFORM THEM IN ANUTTARASAMYAKSAMBODHI, teaching them the Dharma of perfect enlightenment. ALL THESE PEOPLE WILL, BY MEANS OF THIS DHARMA, GRADUALLY ENTER THE BUDDHA PATH. WHY? THE THUS COME ONE'S WISDOM IS HARD TO BELIEVE AND HARD TO UNDERSTAND. Because it is hard to believe, it is difficult to cultivate. Because it is hard to understand, it's difficult to attain the fruit.

Sutra: T. 25 c 12

The living beings, limitless as Ganges' sands, who I transformed at that time are you, yourselves, Bhikshus, and are also those who will be Sound Hearer disciples in the future, after my extinction.

Outline:

> N3. Past and present connections.

Commentary:

THE LIVING BEINGS, LIMITLESS AS GANGES SANDS, WHO I TRANSFORMED AT THAT TIME ARE YOU, YOURSELVES, BHIKSHUS. They are all of you present here, AND ARE ALSO THOSE WHO WILL BE SOUND-HEARER DISCIPLES IN THE FUTURE, AFTER MY EX-TINCTION--disciples of the Sound Hearer Vehicle who will attain the fruits of Arhatship. They are those I taught before.

The Buddhadharma tells us about causes and conditions. If there are no causes, then there are no conditions. Without the cause, there is no effect. For example, before Shakyamuni Buddha became a Buddha, he taught and transformed limitless living beings. Every time. he appeared in the world, he became a Bhikshu and went about everywhere propagating the Buddhadharma. He lectured on the Sutras and spoke the Dharma, and all the living beings believed in him. They thought more of him than they did of their own parents. They felt closer to him than even to themselves! Therefore, they were determined to follow their "Dharma-body parent." Shakyamuni Buddha used his great and equal compassion to teach those living beings. Day by day, their numbers grew, and his fruit position rose higher day by day, as well, until he finally became a Buddha named Shakyamuni. All his students had tremendously deep affinities with him and came to protect the Dharma. Before he became a Buddha, he was also protected by those disciples throughout life after life. They helped him spread the Dharma in every life, right up to and including the lifetime in which he became a Buddha. When he became a Buddha, they all showed up to protect the Dharma. Some didn't show up, however. But they are the ones referred to here in the text "who will be Sound Hearer disciples in the future, after my extinction." Things depend on causes and conditions. So, the Buddha said,

> "All dharmas arise from conditions;
> All dharmas from conditions cease.
> Our teacher, the Buddha, the great Shramana,
> Always teaches it thus."

Sutra: T. 25c14

After my extinction, furthermore, there will be disciples who will not hear this sutra,

who will not know or be aware of the Bod-
hisattva conduct, but who will through the
attainment of their own merit and virtue
give rise to the thought of extinction and
who will enter Nirvana. I shall be a Bud-
dha in another land, with another name.
Although these people will have produced
the thought of extinction and enter into
Nirvana, they will, in those lands, seek
the Buddha's wisdom and get to hear
this sutra and that it is only by means
of the Buddha-vehicle that extinction
can be attained. There are no other ve-
hicles, except for those expedient devices
taught by other Thus Come Ones.

Outline:

N4. Disciples of

the future.

Commentary:

"AFTER MY EXTINCTION," says Shakyamuni Buddha, "when
I have gone to Nirvana, FURTHERMORE, THERE WILL BE DISCI-
PLES, who did not see me when I appeared in the world, WHO
WILL NOT HEAR THIS SUTRA; because they will cultivate the
Dharmas of the Small Vehicle, they will not understand the

wonderful principles of the Great Vehicle. Therefore, they will not hear The Dharma Flower Sutra. ...WHO WILL NOT KNOW OR BE AWARE OF THE BODHISATTVA CONDUCT. They won't know what it is to practice as a Bodhisattva, that is, what Bodhisattvas are supposed to do. BUT WHO WILL, THROUGH THE ATTAINMENT OF THEIR OWN MERIT AND VIRTUE--they may have sat in Dhyana meditation or attained some state, and so will GIVE RISE TO THE THOUGHT OF EXTINCTION AND EN-TER NIRVANA." They will give rise to the thought of the "expedient" fruition and attain the one-sided "Nirvana" of the Arhat, calling it ultimate salvation. They will think, "Oh, I have already passed into extinction. I give rise to no thought at all. I must have entered Nirvana."

I SHALL BE A BUDDHA IN ANOTHER LAND, WITH ANOTHER NAME. I won't be in the Saha world; I'll be in another world. I won't be called Shakyamuni Buddha, either. I'll have another name. ALTHOUGH THESE PEOPLE WILL HAVE PRO-DUCED THE THOUGHT OF EXTINCTION AND ENTRY INTO NIRVANA--although these disciples of the Buddha will have had the false thought that they have entered into Nirvana and at-tained the state of Nirvana, which is beyond production and extinction--THEY WILL, IN THOSE LANDS, SEEK THE BUD-DHA'S WISDOM AND GET TO HEAR THIS SUTRA AND THAT IT IS ONLY BY MEANS OF THE BUDDHA-VEHICLE, the One Buddha Vehicle, THAT EXTINCTION CAN BE ATTAINED. THERE ARE NO OTHER VEHI-CLES, EXCEPT FOR THOSE EXPEDIENT DEVICES TAUGHT BY OTHER THUS COME ONES. The one-sided emptiness of the Sound

Hearers does not count as true extinction. The Dharma Flower Sutra sets forth the One Buddha Vehicle, so that they can enter Nirvana. Sometimes the Buddha will use expedient devices suited for a particular period so he can become enlightened, but these are just expedient devices.

Sutra: T. 25 c 20

Bhikshus, when the Thus Come One knows of himself, that the time of his Nirvana has come, that the assembly is pure, that their faith and understanding are solid and firm, that they fully comprehend the Dharma of emptiness and have deeply entered into Dhyana Samadhi, he will gather together the host of Bodhisattvas and Sound Hearers and speak this sutra for them, saying, "there are not two vehicles by which extinction is attained. There is only the one Buddha vehicle by which extinction can be attained."

Outline:

L2. Still speaking the Dharma Flower.

M1. The time for
speaking.

Commentary:

BHIKSHUS, WHEN THE THUS COME ONE KNOWS OF HIMSELF
THAT THE TIME OF HIS NIRVANA HAS COME, THAT THE ASSEMBLY
IS PURE--all his students have attained purity--and THAT
THEIR FAITH AND UNDERSTANDING ARE SOLID AND FIRM--they won't
be moved; they won't waver--THAT THEY FULLY COMPREHEND THE
DHARMA OF EMPTINESS--they understand that all Dharmas are
empty appearances--AND HAVE DEEPLY ENTERED INTO DHYANA SA-
MADHI, HE WILL GATHER TOGETHER THE HOST OF BODHISATTVAS AND
SOUND HEARERS AND SPEAK THIS SUTRA FOR THEM, The Dharma
Flower Sutra, SAYING, "THERE ARE NOT TWO VEHICLES BY WHICH
EXTINCTION IS ATTAINED.   As far as methods of cultivation
go, one can only gain extinction through the One Buddha Vehicle.   The Two Vehicles may make claims to extinction, but
their extinction is not ultimate.   Those of the Two Vehicles
do not attain extinction.   THERE IS ONLY THE ONE BUDDHA
VEHICLE BY WHICH EXTINCTION CAN BE ATTAINED."   The position
of extinction can be attained only through cultivating the
One Buddha Vehicle.   Other Vehicles will not get you there.

Sutra: T. 25c23
Bhikshus, you should know, the expedients of the Thus Come deeply enter the
natures of living beings. Knowing that

they aspire to and are content with lesser Dharmas and are deeply attached to the five desires, he speaks to them of Nirvana. When they hear him, then they immediately believe and accept it.

Outline:

M2. Three intentions

previously expressed.

Commentary:

BHIKSHUS, YOU SHOULD KNOW, THE EXPEDIENTS OF THE THUS COME ONE DEEPLY ENTER THE NATURES OF LIVING BEINGS. If you started right out teaching living beings the real Dharma, living beings' natures are such that they would not believe it. If you use expedient Dharma-doors, and teach them expediently, they will believe you. The expedient devices of the Buddha are in direct accord with the natures of living beings. Why does he use expedient devices to teach living beings? Because they have their own individual potentials. He speaks according to their individual dispositions. KNOWING THAT THEY ASPIRE TO AND ARE CONTENT WITH LESSER DHARMAS AND ARE DEEPLY ATTACHED TO THE FIVE DESIRES... He knows that they can't see far ahead. All they know is petty things, minor principles. If you spoke to them about the entire universe, they wouldn't understand you. All they know are their own small problems. If you try to talk to them about the big picture, they won't understand you. They like to cultivate on a tiny pathway and are deeply attached to the five desires. They crave wealth, sex, fame, food, and sleep.

Wealth: In this world, money talks. You can get anything with it. Everyone clings to it madly. If you can view money as "empty" then you won't be attached to it. If you can't see it as empty, you'll have to fight for it. I have often told you about the word for money. In Chinese it is 錢 -ch'ien, a word composed of two swords 戈. On the left of the swords stands the radical for gold 金 . This means "You have a sword, and I have a sword, and the two of us fight over the gold." If you have money, you have a lot of problems. If you have no money, you won't have so many problems. But everyone wants money and they aren't afraid of the trouble involved. If you know how to use your money, you can create blessings. If you don't know how to use it, you create offenses. With money you can create merit and virtue, or else you can create offenses. Money is really the worst thing there is! It's also the filthiest thing there is! Haven't you noticed that whenever people count money, they spit on their fingers and then count up the bills? Who knows how many germs are on that money? Quite unsanitary, and yet no one minds. When it comes to money, no one is concerned about hygiene. The desire for money is one thing...

There is also the desire for sex, which includes the

desire for beautiful things.

Everyone wants fame; everyone wants a good reputation. If someone says something bad about you, you feel as hurt as if someone had stuck a knife into your heart. Reputation is very important to people, but it's just one of the five desires.

Everybody likes to eat. If you eat one kind of food for a while, you will start feeling like you'd like something else. You never quite satisfy your desire for food. If you eat one thing, you can't eat another, and so you think about the first kind. If you eat both kinds at the same time, you can't eat enough of either one to get full. In general, there is no way you can ever satisfy your desire for food. If you cultivate the Way, you must not look upon food and drink as so important. You should think of it as medicine that you use to keep your body from falling apart.

The fifth desire is sleep. If you sleep one hour, it's not enough. Two, three, four, five, six hours--you sleep for seven or eight hours and enjoy it immensely. These are the five desires which everyone thinks are so important. Everyone feels that they just can't get along without wealth, sex, fame, food, and sleep.

Once a person asked me a question. He said, "You lecture on so many principles and set forth so many methods. Ultimately, do you know how many people there are in the world? If you know how many people there are in the world,

then I will take refuge with you and you can be my teacher.
But, if you have no exact figures..."

I said, "If you are thinking of taking refuge with me,
basically, I can't answer your questions. Why not? I don't
take disciples with questions like that. If you haven't
taken refuge and you have so many questions, you will have
even more once you take refuge. So, I don't want you for
a disciple. However, I will tell you how many people there
are in this world. In this world there are two people--one
man and one woman. No matter where you go--it's just men
and women. These two people also fit into two categories
based on their behavior. The first seeks fame and the second seeks benefit. Those who seek fame try to think of ways
to get famous. Haven't you seen such people? There are
those who have no fame and try to think of a way to get attention so they fake suicide! They may overdose on sleeping pills, not enough to finish them off, but enough to get
the attention of the police and get their name and pic
ture in the newspaper. "So-and-so tried suicide, is in
serious condition in such-and-such a hospital..." Others,
feeling that faking suicide is too dangerous go out and
try to kidnap someone. All for fame. There are many var-
iations on the publicity game. Those who seek fame get
"burned by the fire." They aren't immune to the flames.
If you can be unattached to a good or bad reputation, then
you can "enter the flames and emerge unburned."

Those who seek benefit think up many plots. They may

sell dope, or engage in various illegal activities. Those who seek benefit "drown in the water." If you seek benefit too energetically, you will drown yourself." So, I answered him that in the world there are only two people. Can you find a third?

He agreed wholeheartedly with me and asked to take refuge. I said, "I won't accept you as a disciple." I put him outside the door, as it were. That was a long time ago...

HE SPEAKS TO THEM OF NIRVANA. To those of the Two Vehicles who delight in lesser dharmas, he teaches the Four Truths and the Twelve Links, so they can attain their "Nirvana." But, actually, it's an expedient device. Those of the Two Vehicles cannot attain Nirvana. WHEN THEY HEAR HIM, THEN THEY IMMEDIATELY BELIEVE AND ACCEPT IT.

Sutra: T. 25 c 27

It is as if, for example, there is a road, five hundred yojanas long, steep, dangerous and bad, an uninhabited and terrifying place. A large group of people wish to travel this road to reach a cache of precious jewels. Among them, there is a guide, intelligent, wise and clear-headed, who knows the road well, both its passable and impassable features...

Outline:

>>> J2. The analogy.

>>>> K1. Setting up the analogy.

>>>>> L1. Analogy of the guide.

Commentary:

IT IS AS IF, FOR EXAMPLE, THERE IS A ROAD. Shakyamuni Buddha says, "I will set up an analogy for you as to why one first teaches people expedient Dharmas and the doctrines of the Two Vehicles...FIVE HUNDRED YOJANAS LONG, STEEP, DANGEROUS, AND BAD. There were thieves on the road, wolves and tigers, it was extremely dangerous. AN UNINHABITED AND TERRIFYING PLACE. Such a long ways, and not a person in sight! Really scary! And suppose A LARGE GROUP OF PEOPLE WISH TO TRAVEL THIS ROAD TO REACH A CACHE OF PRECIOUS JEWELS. The cache of precious jewels represents the highest fruition, that is, Buddhahood. AMONG THEM THERE IS A GUIDE, INTELLIGENT, WISE, AND CLEAR-HEADED. He is intelligent and smart. He knows the way. WHO KNOWS THE ROAD WELL, BOTH ITS PASSABLE AND IMPASSABLE FEATURES. He knows which ways you can walk and which ways are blocked.

Sutra: T. 25c29

And who wishes to lead the group through this hardship.

Outline:

> L2. Wishing to guide
> the followers.
>> M1. Followers be-
>> ing led.

Commentary:

AND WHO WISHES TO LEAD THE GROUP THROUGH THIS HARD-SHIP.   This represents the Buddha teaching those with whom he has affinities, but who have not yet attained liberation. Their past affinities remain, and so they are led by the guide.

Sutra: T. 25 c 29

Midway, the group he is leading grows weary and wishes to turn back. They say to the guide, "we are exhausted and afraid. we cannot go forward. Its too far. We want to turn back now."

Outline:

> M2. Tiring midway
> and wishing to re-
> treat.
>> N1. Retreating
>> from Great Vehicle.

Commentary:

MIDWAY, THE GROUP HE IS LEADING GROWS WEARY AND WISHES TO TURN BACK. The group refers to those of the Two Vehicles. The midway point refers to their lesser "Nirvana." Although they were taught by the Buddha, they are afraid of the Great Vehicle and prefer the smaller vehicle. They are weary and wish to turn back. "THEY SAY TO THE GUIDE," to the Buddha, " WE ARE EXHAUSTED AND AFRAID, we are extremely tired. WE CANNOT GO FORWARD. IT'S TOO FAR. WE WANT TO TURN BACK NOW. We don't want to go forward. We want to turn back. "

Sutra : T. 26 a 2

Their leader, who has many expedients, has this thought; "How pitiful they are. How can they renounce the great and precious treasure and wish to turn back?" Having had this thought, through the power of his expedient devices, he transforms a city in the center of the dangerous road, three hundred yojanas in extent, and says to them,"Do not be afraid. Do not turn back; Stay here now in this great city I have created just for you. If you go into this city, you will be happy

*and at peace. If you then wish to proceed
to the jewel cache, you may do so."*

Outline:

> N2. Leading
>
> those of the
>
> small vehicle.
>
> O1. Exped-
>
> ient set up.

Commentary:

THEIR LEADER, WHO HAS MANY EXPEDIENTS, HAS THIS
THOUGHT, "HOW PITIFUL THEY ARE. HOW CAN THEY RENOUNCE THE
GREAT AND PRECIOUS TREASURE AND WISH TO TURN BACK?" How can
they let go of the great jewel of the Buddha fruit and return? HAVING HAD THIS THOUGHT, THROUGH THE POWER OF HIS
EXPEDIENT DEVICES, HE TRANSFORMS A CITY IN THE CENTER OF
THE DANGEROUS ROAD, THREE HUNDRED YOJANAS IN EXTENT. The
dangerous road is the five paths of rebirth, the five destinies: Humans, gods, hungry ghosts, animals, and hell
beings. Asuras are included in each of the other five.
If you don't become a cow, you become a horse, or if you
don't become a horse, you become a person, or a ghost, or
you fall into the hells. It's extremely dangerous! The
fact that the city is three hundred yojanas in extent represents that one has arrived outside of the three realms
to the land where the sages and common dwell together. He

expediently sets up a city; this is the "Nirvana" of the lesser schools. AND SAYS TO THEM, "DO NOT BE AFRAID. DO NOT TURN BACK; STAY HERE NOW, IN THIS GREAT CITY I HAVE CREATED JUST FOR YOU. I have transformed it just for you, the position of the Two Vehicles. They are not ultimately real, however. Even though the Arhats say they have done what they had to do and will undergo no further becoming, still, their position is not ultimate. IF YOU GO INTO THIS CITY, YOU WILL BE HAPPY AND AT PEACE. You will quickly attain serenity and great peace there. IF YOU THEN WISH TO PROCEED TO THE JEWEL CACHE--if having attained Arhatship you wish to go ahead and cultivate for Buddhahood, you can attain the Buddha fruit--YOU MAY DO SO."

Sutra: T. 26a8

Then the exhausted group rejoiced greatly, having gained what they had never had. "We have now escaped this bad road and gained happiness and peace." Then the group went forward and entered the transformed city; thinking that they had already been saved, they felt happy and at peace.

Outline:

02. Entering

the city in

their joy.

Commentary:

THEN THE EXHAUSTED GROUP REJOICED GREATLY, HAVING GAINED WHAT THEY HAD NEVER HAD. They were extremely tired, when, all of a sudden, a city appeared where they could stop and rest. After cultivating for a while, one may feel very tired. Now, hearing about the rest stop, their minds were filled with joy. They had never seen such a fine city before. The city represents the fruit of the Sound Hearers. " WE HAVE NOW ESCAPED THIS BAD ROAD, we have escaped the paths of the gods, humans, animals, hell-beings, and hungry ghosts--the five evil paths in the Three Realms--AND GAINED HAPPINESS AND PEACE. THEN THE GROUP WENT FORWARD AND ENTERED THE TRANSFORMED CITY; THINKING THAT THEY HAD ALREADY BEEN SAVED, THEY FELT HAPPY AND AT PEACE. They felt they had reached a very high level.

Sutra: T. 26 a 10

At that time, the guide, knowing that they were rested and no longer weary, made the city disappear, saying to them, "All of you, come, let us go. The jewel cache is near. The great city was merely some-

thing I created from transformation to give you a rest."

Outline:

> M3. Making the city
> disappear to lead them
> to the jewel cache.

Commentary:

AT THAT TIME, THE GUIDE, the Buddha, KNOWING THAT THEY WERE RESTED AND NO LONGER WEARY--they'd had their rest and were full of energy again--MADE THE CITY DISAPPEAR, SAYING TO THEM, "ALL OF YOU, COME, LET US GO. THE JEWEL CACHE IS NEAR. We are right near it. " Those of the Sound Hearers who have certified to the Fourth Fruition of Arhatship should go ahead and cultivate the Great Vehicle.

Sutra: T. 26a13

Bhikshus, the Thus Come One is also like this. He now acts as a great guide for all of you. He knows that living beings should leave and cross over the evil road of the torments of birth and death which is so steep, difficult and long.

Outline:

K2. Making the analogy.

L1. Combining.

M1. Analogy of

the guide.

Commentary:

"BHIKSHUS," said Shakyamuni Buddha addressing the four-fold assembly, "THE THUS COME ONE, the Buddha, IS ALSO LIKE THIS, like the principle I spoke above. HE NOW ACTS AS A GREAT GUIDE FOR ALL OF YOU. I am acting as a great leader for all of you, teaching and transforming you. HE KNOWS THAT LIVING BEINGS SHOULD LEAVE AND CROSS OVER THE EVIL ROAD OF THE TORMENTS OF BIRTH AND DEATH; if you are alive, you will have afflictions, troubles, WHICH IS SO STEEP, DIF-FICULT AND LONG." It's a long, hard road. One should get rid of afflictions and cross over birth and death.

Sutra : T. 26a15

If living beings only hear of the one Buddha vehicle, they will not wish to see the Buddha or to draw near to him. Instead, they will think, "the Buddha path is long and far; it can only be accomplished after much labor and suffer-ing." The Buddha knows their minds to be weak and lowly. When they are half-way there, he uses the power of expedients to *speak of the two Nirvanas in order to give them a rest. If living beings dwell on these two levels, the Thus Come One then tells them, "you have not yet finished your job. The level you are dwelling at is near the Buddhas' wisdom. You should observe and ponder this: the Nirvana you have attained is not the real one. The Thus Come One has but used the power of his expedients and, within the one Buddha vehicle, discriminated and spoken of three."*

Outline:

M2. Analogy of

followers.

Commentary:

IF LIVING BEINGS ONLY HEAR OF THE ONE BUDDHA VEHICLE --if I were to start right out speaking The Wonderful Dharma Lotus Flower Sutra, the Dharma-door of the One Buddha Vehicle, THEY WILL NOT WISH TO SEE THE BUDDHA. The Dharma-door of the One Buddha Vehicle is difficult to believe in and difficult to understand. It's not easy to have faith in it or to comprehend it. So, if living beings heard it, they wouldn't want to see the Buddha. They would think, "Cultivating the Buddha Path is entirely too hard." ...OR

TO DRAW NEAR TO HIM, because they are afraid they will lose their grip on the false things they are grasping. If they were to lose the false and gain the true, what would they do? So, they wouldn't want to get near the Buddha. INSTEAD, THEY WILL THINK, "THE BUDDHA PATH IS LONG AND FAR" -- because cultivating the Buddhadharma to become a Buddha takes an incredibly long time. You must pass through three great asankheya aeons! Such a long time. Good grief! That's too much. IT CAN ONLY BE ACCOM- PLISHED AFTER MUCH LABOR AND SUFFERING." Who knows how much hard work is involved, cultivating all the ascetic practices and so on? THE BUDDHA KNOWS THEIR MINDS, Shak- yamuni Buddha and all the Buddhas know the thoughts pass- ing through the minds of living beings. ...TO BE WEAK AND LOWLY. They are weak and soft, not solid at all. As soon as they undergo a bit of opposition, they can't stand it. Lowly means that they are base and stupid. WHEN THEY ARE HALFWAY THERE, HE USES THE POWER OF EXPEDIENTS, clever expedient devices, TO SPEAK OF THE TWO NIRVANAS IN ORDER TO GIVE THEM A REST. They were three hundred yojanas into their five hundred yojana trek. They still had two hundred yojanas to go. Transcending the desire heavens, they trav- elled one hundred yojanas. Transcending to the form realm heavens, they travelled two hundred yojanas. Transcending the formless realm, they travelled three hundred yojanas. Thus, they transcended the three realms. When Bodhisattvas who have transcended the three realms have subdued and destroyed the delusions of dust and sand, they are said to have arrived in the Land of Expedients With Residue, having then travelled four hundred yojanas. If they then break through the delusions of ignorance, they arrive at the Adorned Land of Real Retribution. Then they have travelled five hundred yojanas. They have made it. So, the halfway point is the three hundred yojana mark. The Buddha spoke about the two Nirvanas to give them a rest. The two Nirvanas are 1) with residue, and 2) without residue. Nirvana with residue means that there is something left. This is the Nirvana attained by Arhats who have certified to the fruit and cut off the delusions of views and thought. Their bodies still remain, however. They haven't been able to get rid of both body and wisdom. Nirvana without residue means that you use the real fire of samadhi to annihilate the body as well. You can light your own fire from inside. This is called the annihilation of body and wisdom. But, both these Nirvanas belong to the state of the Two Vehicles.

IF LIVING BEINGS DWELL ON THESE TWO LEVELS, that of Nirvana with residue and Nirvana without residue, THE THUS COME ONE THEN TELLS THEM, "YOU HAVE NOT YET FINISHED YOUR JOB. Your cultivation of the Path is not yet finished. You're not done yet. You've quite a ways to go. THE LEVEL YOU ARE DWELLING AT IS NEAR THE BUDDHAS' WISDOM. YOU SHOULD OBSERVE AND PONDER THIS: THE NIRVANA YOU HAVE ATTAINED IS NOT THE REAL ONE. Both Nirvana with residue and Nirvana without residue are not real; they are not genuine Nirvana.

THE THUS COME ONE HAS BUT USED THE POWER OF HIS EXPEDIENTS
AND, using those clever devices, WITHIN THE ONE BUDDHA VE-
HICLE, DISCRIMINATED AND SPOKEN OF THREE, "the Vehicle of
the Sound Hearers, the Vehicle of the Conditioned Enlightened Ones, and the Bodhisattva Vehicle.

Sutra: T. 26a23

He is like that guide, who, in order to give the travelers a rest, conjured up a great city. Then, when they had rested, he told them, "the place of the jewels is near. This city is not real, but merely something I have conjured up."

Outline:

L2. Drawing the analogy.

Commentary:

HE IS LIKE THAT GUIDE, the Buddha is like the guide
who knows the way through the hazardous road. WHO, IN OR-
DER TO GIVE THE TRAVELERS A REST, knowing that they were
weary, CONJURED UP A GREAT CITY. THEN, WHEN THEY HAD REST-
ED, HE TOLD THEM, "THE PLACE OF THE JEWELS IS NEAR. THIS
CITY IS NOT REAL, BUT MERELY SOMETHING I HAVE CONJURED UP."

Sutra: T. 26 a 25

At that time the World Honored One,
wishing to restate this meaning, spoke
verses saying,

> The Buddha Great-Penetrating-Wisdom-
>   Victory
> Sat in the Bodhimanda for ten aeons,
> Without the manifestation of the Buddha
>   Dharmas,
> And he did not realize the Buddha Way.
> Heavenly spirits and dragon kings,
> And the host of asuras,
> Constantly rained down heavenly flowers,
> As an offering to that Buddha.
> The Gods beat upon their heavenly drums
> And made all kinds of music;
> Fragrant breezes blew away the withered
>   flowers
> And fine, new ones rained down.
> When ten aeons had passed,
> He then realized the Buddha Way.
> All the gods and humans,
> Danced for the joy within their minds.
> The sixteen sons of that Buddha

As well as their retinues,
Thousands of millions surrounding
  them,
All went before that Buddha.
They bowed with their heads at his feet
And asked him to turn the Dharma wheel,
"May the sagely lion's Dharma rain
Fill us and everyone!"

Outline:

> H2. Verses.
>
>> I1. Source of conditions.
>>
>>> J1. Distant conditions.
>>>
>>>> K1. Verses about Great
>>>> Penetrating Wisdom Victory
>>>> becoming a Buddha.

Commentary:

AT THAT TIME, THE WORLD HONORED ONE, WISHING TO RE-
STATE THIS MEANING, SPOKE VERSES SAYING. The Buddha wanted
to go into more detail, so he talked about the doctrines
in verse.

THE BUDDHA GREAT-PENETRATING-WISDOM-VICTORY/ SAT IN
THE BODHIMANDA FOR TEN AEONS/ He sat there in full lotus
in samadhi, but he didn't certify to the fruit in ten
aeons. WITHOUT THE MANIFESTATION OF THE BUDDHADHARMAS/
AND HE DID NOT REALIZE THE BUDDHA WAY/ HEAVENLY SPIRITS

AND DRAGON KINGS/ AND THE HOST OF ASURAS/ the ugly ones, CONSTANTLY RAINED DOWN HEAVENLY FLOWERS/ AS AN OFFERING TO THAT BUDDHA/ to the Buddha Great-Penetrating-Wisdom-Victory.

THE GODS BEAT UPON THEIR HEAVENLY DRUMS/ AND MADE ALL KINDS OF MUSIC/ FRAGRANT BREEZES BLEW AWAY THE WITHERED FLOWERS/ AND FINE, NEW ONES RAINED DOWN/

WHEN TEN AEONS HAD PASSED/ HE THEN REALIZED THE BUDDHA WAY/ The Buddhadharmas manifested, and he realized Anuttara-samyaksambodhi. ALL THE GODS AND HUMANS/ DANCED FOR THE JOY WITHIN THEIR MINDS/ They were all ecstatic. Never had they been so happy.

THE SIXTEEN SONS OF THAT BUDDHA/ AS WELL AS THEIR RETINUES/ THOUSANDS OF MILLIONS SURROUNDING THEM/ ALL WENT BEFORE THAT BUDDHA/

THEY BOWED WITH THEIR HEADS AT HIS FEET/ AND ASKED HIM TO TURN THE DHARMA WHEEL/ "MAY THE SAGELY LION'S DHARMA RAIN/ FILL US AND EVERYONE!"/ Fill us and all living beings.

Sutra: T. 26 b 9

A World Honored One is very hard to
   encounter,
Appearing but once in a long time.
In order to awaken all creatures,
He shakes all things.

Outline:

K2. Ten direction Brahma
kings request Dharma.

L1. His awesome light
shines and shakes all
things.

Commentary:

A WORLD HONORED ONE IS VERY HARD TO ENCOUNTER/ Hard
to encounter as he is, we have now encountered him. AP-
PEARING BUT ONCE IN A LONG TIME/ The Buddha doesn't appear
in every generation. Who knows how long one must have to
wait before a Buddha manifests? IN ORDER TO AWAKEN ALL
CREATURES/ Why does the Buddha manifest in the world? To
wake up all living beings. HE SHAKES ALL THINGS/

Sutra: T. 26 b 11

In five hundred myriads of millions of
lands,
In worlds in the eastern direction,
Brahma palaces shone with a light
Such as they never had before.
The Brahmas, seeing these signs,
Followed them to the Buddha;
They scattered flowers as an offering,
And offered up their palaces,

Asking the Buddha to turn the Dharma wheel,
with verses in his praise.
The Buddha knew the time had not yet come
And received their request seated in silence.
From the other three directions, and four
    points between,
And, likewise, from above, and below,
They scattered flowers and offered their
    palaces,
Asking the Buddha to turn the Dharma
    wheel:
"The World Honored One is very hard
    to meet;
We pray that through his great com-
    passion and pity
He will open wide the sweet dew door
And turn the supreme Dharma wheel."

Outline:

> L2. Brahma Kings come
> to request the Dharma.

Commentary:

IN FIVE HUNDRED MYRIADS OF MILLIONS OF LANDS/ IN
WORLDS OF THE EASTERN DIRECTION/

BRAHMA PALACES SHONE WITH A LIGHT/ SUCH AS THEY NEVER HAD BEFORE/ THE BRAHMAS, SEEING THESE SIGNS/ FOLLOWED THEM TO THE BUDDHA/ When the Great Brahma Kings saw these signs, they followed the light to the Buddha. Ordinarily their palaces shone with light and they wouldn't think light was anything special. But this light was so bright they thought it quite unusual. "Something special is happening." THEY SCATTERED FLOWERS AS AN OFFERING/ The ones they had brought in their flower sacks, very wonderful and fragrant. AND OFFERED UP THEIR PALACES/ ASKING THE BUDDHA TO TURN THE DHARMA WHEEL/ WITH VERSES IN HIS PRAISE/ They scattered heavenly flowers over the Buddha and presented him with their most prized possessions--their palaces. They did this because they wanted him to turn the Dharma Wheel, to speak the Dharma. Before he turned the Dharma Wheel, it was appropriate that they make offerings to him. They praised him with verses.

THE BUDDHA KNEW THE TIME HAD NOT YET COME/ The Buddha Great-Penetrating-Wisdom-Victory knew it wasn't yet time to turn the Wheel. AND RECEIVED THEIR REQUEST SEATED IN SILENCE/ He didn't say a thing. FROM THE OTHER THREE DIRECTIONS, AND FOUR POINTS BETWEEN/ From the south, west, and north and the four intermediate directions, AND, LIKEWISE, FROM ABOVE AND BELOW/ THEY SCATTERED FLOWERS AND OFFERED THEIR PALACES/ ASKING THE BUDDHA TO TURN THE DHARMA WHEEL/

"THE WORLD HONORED ONE IS VERY HARD TO MEET/ It's no simple matter to encounter a Buddha. WE PRAY THAT, THROUGH HIS GREAT COMPASSION AND PITY/ We hope that the Buddha will use his basic wisdom and compassion.

Why does the text say first, the "eastern" direction? Because the east is associated with growth, with wood, and with the season of spring. Therefore, it comes first. The text says, "worlds," plural, because there are many of them. In the east there is the Eastern Crystal World of Medicine Master Buddha, but there are also countless other worlds, as well. In general, they come from "five hundreds of myriads of millions of lands."

HE WILL OPEN WIDE THE SWEET DEW DOOR/ Open wide for all of us the door of sweet dew, the nectar of immortality, so that we may end birth and death. AND TURN THE SUPREME DHARMA WHEEL"/

Sutra: T. 26 b 20

The World Honored One, having limitless wisdom,
Received the multitude's request
And proclaimed various Dharmas for their sakes.
The Four Truths, the Twelve Conditions,
From ignorance up to old age and death —
All arise because of birth.

*In this way the host of calamities comes to be;
you should all know this.
When he expounded on this Dharma
Six hundred myriads of millions of billions
Exhausted the limits of all suffering
And all became Arhats.
When he spoke the Dharma the second time,
Hosts like the sands of a thousand myriads
    of Ganges rivers
Their minds grasping no dharmas,
Also attained Arhatship.
After that, those who gained the Way,
Were incalculable in number;
Were one to count through myriads of mil-
    lions of aeons
One could not reach their limit.*

Outline:

> J2. Verses about that which is
> nearby.
>
>> K1. Verses concerning the
>> turning of the Dharma Wheel
>> of the "half-word" teaching.

Commentary:

THE WORLD HONORED ONE, HAVING LIMITLESS WISDOM/ The

wisdom of the Buddha is boundless. No one's wisdom is greater than the Buddha's. RECEIVED THE MULTITUDES' RE-QUEST/ received the request of all the hundreds of myriads of millions of Brahma Kings and of the sixteen sons. AND PROCLAIMED VARIOUS DHARMAS FOR THEIR SAKES/ He explained all the various Dharma-doors to them. THE FOUR TRUTHS... He began with the Dharma-door of the Four Holy Truths: Suffering, origination, stopping, and the path. ...THE TWELVE CONDITIONS/ Then he preached the Twelve Causal Links. FROM IGNORANCE UP TO OLD AGE AND DEATH/ Ignorance is the first of the twelve, and old age and death comprise the last link. ALL ARISE BECAUSE OF BIRTH/ because of produc-tion. Without birth, none of the other twelve would exist. IN THIS WAY THE HOST OF CALAMITIES COMES TO BE/ all the cares and worries of the world. YOU SHOULD ALL KNOW THIS/ You should all know suffering, cut off origination, long for extinction, and cultivate the Way. WHEN HE EXPOUNDED ON THIS DHARMA/ When the Buddha Great-Penetrating-Wisdom-Victory spoke the Four Truths and the Twelve Links, SIX HUNDRED MYRIADS OF MILLIONS OF BILLIONS/ EXHAUSTED THE LIMITS OF ALL SUFFERING/ All their sufferings were over, AND ALL BECAME ARHATS/

WHEN HE SPOKE THE DHARMA THE SECOND TIME/ The first speaking here refers to the Agama Period of the Buddha's teaching. The second speaking refers to the Vaipulya Per-iod. HOSTS LIKE THE SANDS OF A THOUSAND MYRIADS OF GANGES RIVERS/ THEIR MINDS GRASPING NO DHARMAS/ This means that their minds took in no unwholesome dharmas, no dharmas of affliction, ALSO ATTAINED ARHATSHIP/ They certified to the Fourth Fruit of Arhatship. AFTER THAT, THOSE WHO GAINED THE WAY/ Those who went from Arhatship on to the Bodhisattva Path, WERE INCALCULABLE IN NUMBER/ You couldn't count them; no way. ONE COULD NOT REACH THEIR LIMIT/ This Buddha saved an uncountable number of beings. They could never be counted.

Sutra: T. 26 c 2

At that time, the sixteen princes,
Left home and became Shramaneras.
Together they requested that the Buddha
Extensively proclaim the Dharma of the
    Great Vehicle :
"May we and our followers
All perfect the Buddha Way.
We wish to become like the World Honored One,
With the wisdom Eye and foremost purity."
The Buddha, knowing the intentions of the
    youths,
Their practices in former lives,
Used limitless causes and conditions
And various analogies,

To teach them the six paramitas,
As well as matters of spiritual penetra-
tions.
He discriminated the real Dharma,
And the pathway walked by the Bodhi-
sattvas.
He spoke the Dharma Flower Sutra
Its verses in numbers like Gange's sands.
After that Buddha had spoken the sutra
In a quiet room he entered Dhyana Samadhi
Single-mindedly sitting in one place,
For eighty-four thousand aeons.

Outline:

K2. Verses concerning the
turning of the Dharma Wheel
which dispenses with the
half-word teaching and
clarifies the full-word
teaching.

Commentary:

AT THAT TIME, THE SIXTEEN PRINCES/ the sixteen sons of
the Buddha Great-Penetrating-Wisdom-Victory, LEFT HOME AND
BECAME SHRAMANERAS/ A shramanera is a novice monk. Novices
take ten precepts. TOGETHER THEY REQUESTED THAT BUDDHA/

the Buddha Great-Penetrating-Wisdom-Victory, TO EXTENSIVELY
PROCLAIM THE DHARMA OF THE GREAT VEHICLE/ to speak The Won-
derful Dharma Lotus Flower Sutra. They said "MAY WE AND
OUR FOLLOWERS/ ALL PERFECT THE BUDDHA WAY/ May we all be-
come Buddhas. WE WISH TO BECOME LIKE THE WORLD HONORED
ONE/ We want to be exactly like the Buddha. WITH THE WIS-
DOM EYE AND FOREMOST PURITY"/ The Buddha possesses the Eye
of wisdom and is ultimately pure.

THE BUDDHA, KNOWING THE INTENTIONS OF THE YOUTHS/ knowing the thoughts of his sixteen sons. A "youth" is a child
who is still a virgin. THEIR PRACTICES IN FORMER LIVES/
He knew what kind of practices they had previously engaged
in. USED LIMITLESS CAUSES AND CONDITIONS/ AND VARIOUS ANAL-
OGIES/ TO TEACH THEM THE SIX PARAMITAS/ Giving, morality,
patience, vigor, concentration, and wisdom. Paramita is a
Sanskrit word which means "arrived at the other shore." AS
WELL AS MATTERS OF SPIRITUAL PENETRATIONS/

HE DISCRIMINATED THE REAL DHARMA/ AND THE PATHWAY
WALKED BY THE BODHISATTVAS/ He defined the real, genuine
Buddhadharma and the Bodhisattva path.

HE SPOKE THE DHARMA FLOWER SUTRA/ The Sutra of the
Great Vehicle, The Wonderful Dharma Lotus Flower Sutra. ITS
VERSES IN NUMBER LIKE GANGES' SANDS/ AFTER THAT BUDDHA HAD
SPOKEN THE SUTRA/ After the Buddha Great-Penetrating-Wisdom-
Victory had spoken the Sutra, IN A QUIET ROOM, HE ENTERED
DHYANA SAMADHI/ He went to his room and entered samadhi.
SINGLE-MINDEDLY SITTING IN ONE PLACE/ He meditated there
FOR EIGHTY-FOUR THOUSAND AEONS/

1370

Sutra: T. 26c13

All the Shramaneras,
Knowing the Buddha had not yet left Dhyana,
For the sake of the limitless millions assem-
    bled,
Spoke of the Buddha's unsurpassed wisdom.
Each seated on his Dharma throne,
Spoke this Great Vehicle Sutra.
After the Buddha had become peacefully
    still,
They propagated and taught the Dharma.
Each one of the Shramaneras
Took across living beings
To the number of grains of sand
In six hundred myriads of Ganges rivers.

Outline:

> I2. Tying up conditions.
>> J1. Speaking of Dharma.
>>> K1. Verses about their
>>> former affinities in common.

Commentary:

ALL THE SHRAMANERAS/ the sixteen Shramaneras and the
Arhats, KNOWING THE BUDDHA HAD NOT YET LEFT DHYANA/ FOR THE
SAKE OF THE LIMITLESS MILLIONS ASSEMBLED/ for all the liv-

ing beings, SPOKE OF THE BUDDHA'S UNSURPASSED WISDOM/
taught the supreme wisdom of the Buddha. EACH SEATED ON
HIS DHARMA THRONE/ Each of the sixteen princes took their
Dharma-seat and SPOKE THIS GREAT VEHICLE SUTRA/ The Wonder-
ful Dharma Lotus Flower Sutra. AFTER THE BUDDHA HAD BE-
COME PEACEFULLY STILL/ THEY PROPAGATED AND TAUGHT THE
DHARMA/ They spread the teachings of the Buddha. EACH ONE
OF THE SHRAMANERAS/ the sixteen, TOOK ACROSS LIVING BEINGS/
TO THE NUMBER OF GRAINS OF SAND/ IN SIX HUNDRED MYRIADS OF
MILLIONS OF GANGES RIVERS/

Someone has heard the word Arhat and wondered what it
means. Those who listen to Sutra lectures often will know,
but those who are new won't. Arhat is a Sanskrit word
which is interpreted in three ways, "Worthy of Offerings,"
"Destroyer of Evil," and "Killer of Thieves." Arhats are
worthy of receiving offerings from gods and humans. If no
one makes offerings to them, they won't force people. They
just return the light and say, "Probably in former lives
I didn't cultivate blessings. As a result, now my bowl is
empty." As "destroyers of evil" they have wiped out the
evils of affliction. As "killers of thieves" they have
killed the thief of ignorance. Ignorance is a thief who
ruins one's Way karma. Why do people do confused things?
They do them out of ignorance. Why do people do things
that are upside-down? It's out of ignorance. Why is it
that, when one has no attachments, one deliberately looks
for attachments? It's all out of ignorance. In spite of

the fact that it is in our power to end birth and death, why do we fail to do so? Because of ignorance. So, ignorance is just terrible! Arhats kill ignorance. While we say they "kill" ignorance, they haven't killed it entirely. They have killed coarse ignorance, but a subtle ignorance remains. Ignorance could be likened to a virus. Perhaps you break out in a sore. When you put some medicine on it, it clears up. But, as soon as you quit applying the medicine, it breaks out again, and your skin itches like crazy. The Arhats have the medicine and put it on the sore, but they haven't gotten rid of the disease at it's source. The only way to get rid of it entirely is to become a Buddha. I have told you before many times that even Bodhisattvas at the level of Equal Enlightenment still have one share of production-mark ignorance which they haven't severed. Arhats have ignorance, and so do the Bodhisattvas. They don't use their ignorance, that's all. Ignorance is stupidity. If the Equal Enlightenment Bodhisattvas break through that last remaining part of stupidity, they become Buddhas. Because the word Arhat encompasses all these meanings, we retain the Sanskrit word and do not translate it.

Sutra: T. 26c19

> After that Buddha had crossed over into
>   extinction,
> All those who   heard the Dharma,

In whatever Buddhalands they might be,
Were reborn there together with their
teachers.

Outline:

> K2. Meeting with one another
> during the time in between.

Commentary:

AFTER THAT BUDDHA HAD CROSSED OVER INTO EXTINCTION/
ALL THOSE WHO HAD HEARD THE DHARMA/ After the Buddha Great-
Penetrating-Wisdom-Victory had gone to final Nirvana, all
those who had heard the Dharma, IN WHATEVER BUDDHALANDS
THEY MIGHT BE/ WERE REBORN THERE TOGETHER WITH THEIR TEACH-
ERS/ Those who had heard the Dharma from one of the sixteen
Shramaneras were reborn together with their teacher in
other Buddhalands.

Sutra: T. 26c 21
The sixteen Shramaneras
Perfectly practiced the Buddha Path.
Presently in the ten directions
Each has realized proper enlightenment.
Those who heard the Dharma then,
Are each in the presence of a Buddha;
Those who are Sound Hearers,

Are gradually taught the Buddha Path.
I was one of the sixteen;
In the past, I taught all of you.
I therefore use expedients
To draw you into the Buddha's wisdom.

Outline:

> > K3. Dharma Flower still
> > being spoken.
> > > L1. The Assembly past
> > > and present.

Commentary:

THE SIXTEEN SHRAMANERAS/ the sixteen sons of the Buddha Great-Penetrating-Wisdom-Victory, PERFECTLY PRACTICED THE BUDDHA PATH/ All those shramaneras perfect the cultivation of the Buddha Path. PRESENTLY IN THE TEN DIRECTIONS/ Now, in the worlds of the ten directions, EACH HAS REALIZED PROPER ENLIGHTENMENT/ Through their cultivation of the Buddha path they have realized the fruits of Buddhahood.

THOSE WHO HEARD THE DHARMA THEN/ Those who heard the Dharma proclaimed at that time, ARE EACH IN THE PRESENCE OF A BUDDHA/ They have reappeared each in the place where his former teacher became a Buddha. They went along with their teachers, each one of them. THOSE WHO ARE SOUND HEARERS/ ARE GRADUALLY TAUGHT THE BUDDHA PATH/ Those lacking strength, who have settled for a position of Sound

Hearer, are gradually, bit-by-bit, instructed by means of the Buddha Path. They are led by degrees to the supreme Buddha Vehicle.

I WAS ONE OF THE SIXTEEN/ I, myself, Shakyamuni Buddha, was one of the sixteen shramaneras. IN THE PAST, I TAUGHT ALL OF YOU/ You assembled here now listening to me speak The Dharma Flower Sutra--you all listened to me speak it then, way back in the distant past.

I THEREFORE USE EXPEDIENTS/ TO DRAW YOU INTO THE BUDDHA'S WISDOM/ Because you delight in lesser dharmas, I employ expedient devices to lead you to the Buddha's supreme wisdom.

Sutra: T. 26 c27

Through these former causal conditions,
I presently speak The Dharma Flower
*   Sutra,*
Leading you to enter the Buddha Path.
Take care not to become frightened.

Outline:

L2. Certifying that he is now speaking the Dharma Flower.

Commentary:

THROUGH THESE FORMER CAUSAL CONDITIONS/ It is by means

of the former connection I just told you about that I PRES--
ENTLY SPEAK THE DHARMA FLOWER SUTRA/ LEADING YOU TO ENTER
THE BUDDHA PATH/ TAKE CARE NOT TO BECOME FRIGHTENED/ You are
about to hear the Great Vehicle, genuine Dharma. Do not become alarmed. Here, I will set forth an analogy to make it
even clearer:

Sutra: T. 26c29
　Suppose there is a steep and bad road,
　Remote and teeming with venomous beasts,
　Lacking, as well, water or grass
　-A place feared by all.
　Countless thousands of myriads
　Wish to traverse this dangerous road
　With its pathways so distant,
　Extending five hundred yojanas.
　There is among them a guide,
　Intelligent and wise,
　Clear and resolute in mind,
　Who can rescue them from their difficulty.

Outline:

J1. Verses about parable.

K1. Setting up parable.

L1. Verses about the
guide.

Commentary:

SUPPOSE THERE IS A STEEP AND BAD ROAD/ a very dangerous and evil road. What is this steep and bad road? It is the turning wheel of the six paths of rebirth. REMOTE AND TEEMING WITH VENOMOUS BEASTS/ It is remote. No one traverses it. There are many deadly beasts there, too. Evil beasts and venomous snakes. There are tigers, lions, wolves, and panthers, too. LACKING, AS WELL, WATER OR GRASS/ Not only was it dangerous, there wasn't even any water or any grass. Obviously, there was nothing to eat. A PLACE FEARED BY ALL/ Everyone was scared of this road. COUNTLESS THOUSANDS OF MYRIADS/ WISH TO TRAVERSE THIS DANGEROUS ROAD/ people want to travel on this road, to cross the six paths of rebirth. WITH ITS PATHWAYS SO DISTANT/ Living beings want to transcend the three realms, to get off the six paths of rebirth, to cultivate and become Buddhas. However, the road to Buddhahood is far indeed, very distant. EXTENDING FIVE HUNDRED YOJANAS/ Such a long ways one has to go to the Buddhaland! Transcending the realm of desire equals traveling one hundred yojanas. Transcending the world of form equals traveling two hundred yojanas. Transcending the formless world equals traveling three hundred yojanas. Then, breaking through the delusions like dust and sand equals traveling four hundred yojanas. Breaking through delusions of ignorance, the most subtle of delusions, equals traveling five hundred yojanas. With no one to guide you, it is hard indeed to travel this road.

THERE IS AMONG THEM A GUIDE/ someone to lead them. INTELLIGENT AND WISE/ "Intelligent" here means that he had a good memory. He wasn't absent-minded. He is knowledgeable and remembers it always. He was wise as a result of his learning. CLEAR AND RESOLUTE IN MIND/ He knew what was going on. He had excellent, unfailing judgment. He would be able to lead them down the right road. WHO CAN RESCUE THEM FROM THEIR DIFFICULTY/ He can save all living beings from their sufferings on the hard road of birth and death.

Sutra: T. 27 a 6

The group grows weary
And says to the guide,
"We are all exhausted, now
And want to turn back."

Outline:

> L2. Verses about followers.
>> M1. Followers want to retreat halfway.
>>> N1. The multitude retreats from the great.

Commentary:

THE GROUP GROWS WEARY/ It is very difficult to culti-

vate on such a dangerous path. The aiding conditions are
scarce and the opposing conditions are many. What are "aiding conditions?" For example, if you cultivate and don't
have the strength to keep going, then your Good Knowing Advisor helps you. He tells you not to go down the wrong road.
He advises you not to indulge in impure thinking. Then, you
cultivate according to his advice and that is an aiding condition. Also, if you don't have the strength to complete a
task in cultivation, the Dharma Protectors may come to your
aid.

What are opposing conditions? Say you want to cultivate, and you bring forth a very true Bodhi-mind, but then
someone comes along and uses all kinds of devious tricks to
ruin your cultivation and cripple your Bodhi-mind. Originally you had no lust, but this person inflames your lust.
Originally, your Way-mind was very solid, but this person
stunts its growth. These are opposing conditions. The Way
is very difficult to cultivate. Sometimes one grows weary--
sick and tired, you might say. You cultivate for one year--
no success. You cultivate for two years, and still nothing
is obtained. By the end of the third year, "God," you say,
"I've been wasting my time. Cultivation is impossible!" and
you retreat, exhausted.

AND SAYS TO THE GUIDE/ to the Good Knowing Advisor,
"WE ARE ALL EXHAUSTED NOW/ worn out. I've been cultivating and enduring all this pain, and I've not gotten a single thing out of it. I've gotten exactly nowhere, as a

matter of fact.   ...AND WANT TO TURN BACK.   That does it;
we quit!"

Sutra: T. 27a8
　The guide thinks to himself,
　"How very pitiful they are.
　How can they wish to turn back
　And lose the great and precious treasure?"
　Instantly he thinks of a device :
　Using the power of spiritual penetrations
　He conjures up a great city
　Adorned with houses,
　Surrounded by gardens and groves,
　Brooks and bathing ponds,
　Layered gates and tiered pavilions,
　Filled with men and women.
　After creating this,
　He pities them saying, "Do not be afraid.
　But go into this city
　And enjoy yourselves as you wish."

Outline:

N2. Guide in-

duces the small.

01. The de-
vice is con-
jured up.

Commentary:

THE GUIDE THINKS TO HIMSELF/ "HOW VERY PITIFUL THEY
ARE"/ They are to be pitied, really. Why? They cultivate
and are exactly one hairsbreadth away from realization and
then want to turn back. As soon as they retreat, they
lose all their former work. "HOW CAN THEY WISH TO TURN
BACK/ AND LOSE THE GREAT AND PRECIOUS TREASURE"/ You retreat and in so doing lose all the wonderful treasure that
was coming to you. INSTANTLY HE THINKS OF A DEVICE:/ USING
THE POWER OF SPIRITUAL PENETRATIONS/ HE CONJURES UP A GREAT
CITY/ ADORNED WITH HOUSES/ SURROUNDED BY GARDENS AND GROVES/
a lovely place indeed, with inner and outer walls, many
fine buildings, lots of running brooks and ponds. BROOKS
AND BATHING PONDS/ LAYERED GATES AND TIERED PAVILIONS/ high
and lofty buildings. AND FILLED WITH MEN AND WOMEN/ a lot
of people.

AFTER CREATING THIS/ HE PITIES THEM, SAYING, "DO NOT
BE AFRAID/ BUT GO INTO THIS CITY/ AND ENJOY YOURSELVES AS
YOU WISH"/ Do what you like. The transformation city represents the Nirvana with residue of the Two Vehicles. The
Buddha used this device to draw in the Sound Hearers, saying, "When you gain fourth stage Arhatship, you have ended
birth and death, finished your work. No further becoming

for you. That is true happiness." Then, once they had
attained the fourth fruit, he told them they had to go further, to the treasure trove. The Transformation City is
the place of the Two Vehicles. In the Dharma Flower Assembly the Buddha opens the provisional and reveals the real
teaching, telling everyone the transformation city is not
real. Before you reach the level of the transformation
city, you can't say it is not real. But, once you get there,
then you know it is, and you must go on.

Sutra: 27a 16

> When they had entered the city,
> They rejoiced greatly at heart
> Thinking they were safe and sound,
> And that they had been saved.

Outline:

02. They go
forward joy-
fully and en-
ter the City.

Commentary:

WHEN THEY HAD ENTERED THE CITY/ Those of the small vehicle liked the small vehicle dharmas, so they went right
into the transformed city. The transformed city represents
the fruit positions of the small vehicle. THEY REJOICED

GREATLY AT HEART/ THINKING THEY WERE SAFE AND SOUND/ They felt happy and at ease, thinking that they had already ended birth and death and attained Nirvana. AND THAT THEY HAD BEEN SAVED/ had been taken across the suffering sea of birth and death.

Sutra: T. 27 a 18

The guide, knowing they were rested,
Assembled them together and said,
"You should all go forward,
For this is nothing but a transformed
    city.
Seeing that you were exhausted
And wanted to turn back midway,
I used the power of expedients,
To transform provisionally this city.
You should now be vigorous
And proceed to the jewel cache."

Outline:

M2. He destroys the transformation to lead them to the jewel cache.

Commentary:

THE GUIDE, KNOWING THEY WERE RESTED/ The guide, the

great Good Knowing Advisor, in this case the Buddha, knowing that those of the Two Vehicles had reached their small
vehicle destinations and that they were satisfied with
that, ASSEMBLED THEM TOGETHER AND SAID/ "YOU SHOULD ALL
GO FORWARD/ Now you have rested and you are no longer
tired; you have certified to the position of the Two Vehicles. You are pretty happy about that, aren't you? But
you shouldn't stay in the Two Vehicle Nirvana. You have
to go forward. FOR THIS IS NOTHING BUT A TRANSFORMED CITY/
It's not real. It's not the jewel cache. It's simply
something I created.

"SEEING THAT YOU WERE EXHAUSTED/ You had been working
very hard, AND WANTED TO TURN BACK MIDWAY/ You felt you
had undergone too much suffering. This is like when we
cultivate for one, two days, it's not so bad. But, after
a while, one feels as if one had not attained anything and
gets discouraged and wants to retreat. They think, "I cultivated a whole year, two whole years, and I haven't become a Buddha yet. Why? I've been here two years, and I
haven't been enlightened. I wonder if it's ever possible
to get enlightened? Am I being cheated by this idea of
enlightenment?" In this way, one's mind becomes filled
with doubts, and one quits cultivating.

Everyone here eats one meal a day. Even if you wanted
to steal food at other times, there's no place to steal it
from! It's too bitter. So you want to turn back midway.
Right? "If I had known it was so bitter, I wouldn't have

left home. I really got cheated. I did! What a bad teacher! What am I going to do?"

When the guide saw that they were so tired, he "USED THE
POWER OF EXPEDIENTS / He said, "Don't get nervous. You'll
get enlightened tomorrow. Just work one more night." So,
they go ahead and cultivate one more night. Then he says,
"You're off just a bit. Just a hair. Keep trying." So,
he keeps them cultivating bit-by-bit. All of a sudden, his
life has come to an end. Although he didn't get enlightened,
he almost did. Probably, he will for sure next life. So
next life, he studies the Buddhadharma again.

"TO TRANSFORM PROVISIONALLY THIS CITY / He used clever
expedients to set up the Dharma-doors of the Two Vehicles.

"YOU SHOULD NOW BE VIGOROUS/ Now you have rested. You
should be courageous and press on in your cultivation. AND
PROCEED TO THE JEWEL CACHE/ I will go along with you to the
Buddha fruit. You will certainly become Buddhas." If the
Buddha had told the Two Vehicles to cultivate the Buddha
fruit from the beginning, they wouldn't have believed him.
They wouldn't have believed that they could become Buddhas.

Sutra: T.27a23
  I, too, am like this,
  I am the guide of all;

Outline:

> > K2. Drawing analogy to
> > Dharma.
> > > L1. Comparison.
> > > > M1. Guide.

Commentary:

Shakyamuni Buddha says, I, TOO, AM LIKE THIS/ "I am the same." I AM THE GUIDE OF ALL/ "I am a Good Knowing Advisor for all living beings. I teach all living beings to hurry up and become Buddhas."

Sutra: T. 27 a 23

Seeing those who seek the way,
Exhausted in mid-course
Unable to cross the dangerous paths,
Of birth, death and affliction,
Therefore, I use the power of expedients,
To speak of Nirvana and give them a rest,
Saying, "Your sufferings are ended.
You have done what you had to do.
Then, knowing they have reached Nirvana,
And had all become Arhats,
I gather them together,
To teach them the genuine Dharma.
The Buddhas use the power of expedients,

To discriminate and speak of three vehicles
But there is only the one Buddha Vehicle.
The other two were spoken as a resting
 place.
What I am telling you now is the truth;
What you have gained is not extinction.
For the sake of the Buddha's all wisdom,
you should exert yourselves with great
 vigor.
When you have certified to all wisdom,
And have the Ten Powers and other
 Buddha Dharmas
And have perfected the thirty-two marks,
Then that is genuine extinction.

Outline:

> M2. Followers.

Commentary:

SEEING THOSE WHO SEEK THE WAY/ EXHAUSTED IN MID-COURSE/ They cultivate, and when they are half-way there, they decide they can't cultivate anymore. They can't stand the suffering. They get tired and slack off. So it's said,

The first year you cultivate, the Buddha's
right in front of you.
By the third year, he's eighty-thousand
miles away.
By the tenth year, he's completely out
of sight.

When you first decide to cultivate, you may be very sincere. If you could have held on to that kind of sincerity, you would have become a Buddha by now. However, you can't keep it up for very long. Half way there you get lazy. This is like, here, some people should have already opened the five eyes and gained the six spiritual penetrations. Why haven't they done so? It's because they are lazy. Some people have opened the five eyes and gained the six penetrations, but haven't developed any genuine wisdom. This is also because they are lazy and they haven't purified themselves of desire. Some people have the five eyes and six spiritual penetrations, but then they get lazy and fail to cultivate and lose their powers. These are all cases of turning back exhausted at the half-way point.

UNABLE TO CROSS THE DANGEROUS PATHS/ OF BIRTH, DEATH, AND AFFLICTION/ Unable to cross the sea of suffering, unable to cross the most dangerous road of affliction. THERE-FORE I USE THE POWER OF EXPEDIENTS/ expedient dharma-doors, TO SPEAK OF NIRVANA AND GIVE THEM A REST/ To let the cultivators have a rest, he lets them have their Nirvana with residue. SAYING, "YOUR SUFFERINGS ARE ENDED"/ I say, "Your suffering is all gone. YOU HAVE DONE WHAT YOU HAD TO DO/ Your job is done." THEN, KNOWING THEY HAVE REACHED NIRVANA/ AND HAD ALL BECOME ARHATS/ I GATHER THEM TOGETHER/ TO TEACH THEM THE GENUINE DHARMA/ I open the provisional to reveal the real and teach the real Dharma, The Dharma Flower Sutra. We are now hearing the Dharma of The Lotus Sutra, so we should put forth vigor. We should not linger in Transformation City.

THE BUDDHAS USE THE POWER OF EXPEDIENTS/ The Buddhas of the ten directions and the three periods of time teach and transform living beings using expedient means. TO DISCRIMINATE AND SPEAK OF THREE VEHICLES/ The Buddhadharma, in reality, is only the One Buddha Vehicle. The Sound Hearer, Conditioned Enlightened Ones, and the Bodhisattva Vehicles do not really exist. If at the beginning, the Buddha had talked about the Buddha Vehicle, living beings would have been afraid. So, the Buddhas set forth the provisional dharmas for the sake of the real. Although they speak provisional dharmas, their ultimate destination is still the real Dharmas. So it says, "They discriminate and speak of Three Vehicles." Fearing living beings would think the Buddha fruit was too far away and they could never cultivate it successfully, they decided to speak the Three Vehicles to lead living beings there gradually. BUT THERE IS ONLY THE ONE BUDDHA VEHICLE/ The Three Vehicles are just Transformation City. They are transformed by the Buddha's spiritual power. In the future, living beings will attain the Buddha fruit, for there is only the One Real Buddha Vehicle. THE OTHER TWO WERE SPOKEN AS A RESTING PLACE/ The Buddha saw that living beings had been cultivating for such a long time that they were discouraged. Consequently, he magically created the city so they could rest up a bit. The Buddha spoke of the two kinds of Nirvana: with residue and without residue.

WHAT I AM TELLING YOU NOW IS THE TRUTH/ "You should go beyond the Transformation City. I am telling you the real Dharma, the Buddha Vehicle." WHAT YOU HAVE GAINED IS NOT EXTINCTION/ "The Nirvana with residue that you have attained, the Fourth Fruit of Arhatship, is not Buddhahood. It's not ultimate; it's not real extinction. You haven't completely ended birth and death and attained the bliss of still extinction. You still have a ways to go." As Fourth Stage Arhats, they have ended Share Section birth and death, but they have not yet ended Change birth and death.

Share Section birth and death refers to our physical existence, that is, every person has his own body which exists for a certain period of time. Change birth and death refers to the continual process of birth and death of thoughts in our minds.

FOR THE SAKE OF THE BUDDHAS' ALL WISDOM/ the wisdom of real mark Prajna, YOU SHOULD EXERT YOURSELVES WITH VIGOR/ You should be extremely vigorous and seek Prajna wisdom.

Don't stop at Fourth Stage Arhatship and fail to go forward.
WHEN YOU HAVE CERTIFIED TO ALL WISDOM/ real wisdom, AND
HAVE THE TEN POWERS AND OTHER BUDDHA DHARMAS/ The Ten Powers have been explained before. I shall now elaborate on
a few of them, not all ten. The second is, "The Buddha
knows the karmic retribution of living beings in the three
periods of time." For now, we won't talk about the three
periods of time. We will talk about yesterday, today, and
tomorrow. Or, we can talk about last month, this month,
and next month, or we can talk about last year, this year,
and next year. If you don't believe that there are future
lives or past lives, you only believe in this life. So I
will change the time period. Surely you will admit to the
concept of last year, this year, and next year. You can't
disagree with that. If you can't, then you can't really
object to the idea of past, present, and future lives. The
Buddha knows the karmic retribution of living beings--that
is, what karmic offenses or good deeds they did in past
lives, and what their cause and effect is. They know cur-
rently what they are undergoing as retribution. They also
know the fruits they will reap in the future.

The fourth is that the Buddha knows the superiority or
inferiority of living beings' faculties. This means he
knows which living beings have good roots and which do not.
The Buddha knows at a glance. The Buddha knows, but he
won't tell you. He won't blast a living being saying,
"You are too rotten. Hurry up and get away from the Bud-

dha!" He wouldn't say that. He also wouldn't say, "Oh, you have such fine, good roots. You should draw near to the Buddha." He won't talk about these things. Why not? It's one thing to know about them; it's another thing to broadcast your knowledge. You can't go around telling people all these things. You may know, but you <u>can't</u> tell. If you tell living beings they have good roots, they will get arrogant, thinking it doesn't matter if they cultivate or not. Then you have harmed them. Those without good roots should not be told either, or they will get discouraged and refuse to cultivate. Thinking it meaningless, they will retreat. If they don't know whether or not they have good roots, they will go ahead and cultivate. If they know, they will be lazy and retreat from the Bodhi mind. The Buddha knows, but he doesn't tell people. He's not like common people who don't know, but press the issue and insist that they do know. The Buddha knows, but doesn't tell. We don't know and stupidly claim we do.

Genuinely intelligent people would never say, "See me? I am the most intelligent person there is!" People who say they are smart are already stupid to the extreme. If they weren't stupid, they wouldn't praise themselves as being wise. Some people affect very strange styles and ways of thinking. If you flatter them with even one sentence of praise, they feel it's as sweet as eating honey. If you say one thing unfavorable, they find it bitter as gall. Praise them, and they are delighted. If you don't praise them, they will praise themselves. No one else praises them, so they have to introduce themselves. They say, "I cultivate real hard. I have made a lot of progress. I have no false thinking." How do you know you have no false thinking? If you know you have no false thinking, that itself is false thinking. If you had no false thinking, you wouldn't have to introduce yourself and say, "I have no false thinking." Why do you want everyone to know that you have no false thinking? Others cultivate and claim that they have no thoughts of sexual desire. As soon as you say you don't have desire, that means you do have it. If you really didn't have any desire, you wouldn't feel compelled to say that you didn't. If you don't have any, why bring it up in the first place? If you bring it up, that means it's still there. You just want to give yourself a high hat to wear and to cheat people into thinking that you have no sexual desire. I will tell you, until you have reached Fourth Stage Arhatship, you can't say that you have no sexual desire.

"Oh, in that case then I probably have certified to the fourth fruit, because I really don't have any. You just don't believe me, that's all." If you really didn't have any, why would you be worried about people believing that you did or didn't? Hmm? If you don't, you don't. Why try to get people to believe you? Huh? If other people believe that you don't have any, that's not going to help them get rid of theirs! It doesn't work like that.

So, what's the big deal?

There are a lot of people who speak out of both sides of their mouths. They say they do, and they say they don't. For example, they don't have the Buddha's wisdom, but then they say that they do. They aren't as pure as the Buddha, but they say that they are. Living beings all like to be number one. They even want to put the Buddha in the number two slot! So, the fourth wisdom power of the Buddha is knowing the superiority or inferiority of living beings' dispositions.

The fifth wisdom power is to know the various capacities of understanding of living beings. Not only does one understand oneself, but one understands other living beings as well. If you only understand yourself and know how to lecture the Sutras, what good does that do anyone else? If you can lecture the Sutras, but living beings can't understand it, it's useless. You have to be aware of what living beings can understand, so that when you explain a certain principle, a certain living being can understand it, and if you explain another principle, that other living being can understand it. You can't explain things too profoundly or too mysteriously so people can't understand. If they don't understand, it may be very profound, but it's of no use. Right? The doctrines must be explained so that everyone can understand and accept them. That's one of the powers of the Buddha. He knows what living beings can understand, and he teaches them accordingly. You shouldn't lecture on purpose

so that people can't understand you. It would be better
not to lecture at all than to do that.

The sixth wisdom power is that the Buddha knows all
the different states of living beings. Everyone has their
own state of mind. Everyone has their fondnesses and their
dislikes. Some living beings like to eat sweet things.
Some don't. Some like bitter things, sour things, hot
things... There are many different religions in the world,
too. There's Confucianism, Taoism, Buddhism, Christianity,
Islam. They are like the different flavors. Everybody has
their preference. If you look at it one way, there are
many different religions. If you look at it another way,
they are all included in Buddhism. No religion is outside
of Buddhism. Other religions claim that they are the
truest, the most lofty. Buddhism doesn't claim to be lofty, or true, because all religions, true or false, high or
low--all are included within Buddhism. None of them are
outside of Buddhism. The true is Buddhism, and the false
is Buddhism. They are all included within Buddhism. True
and false, high and low, are discriminations made by living beings; there are no such discriminations within the
religion itself. As The Vajra Sutra says, "This Dharma is
level and equal, with nothing above or below it." Where
is this "true and false?" The true comes from the false,
and the false comes from the true. It's just like day and
night. When the day reaches its ultimate, night is falling.
When night reaches its ultimate, dawn is breaking. People

are awake sometimes, and sometimes they are asleep. When
they are asleep, they don't know anything at all. When
they are awake, they are alert. When they sleep they dream.
The dreams are false. Religions are a bit like this. It's
not that religions are always alert and awake. Sometimes
they are sleeping, too. When religions are asleep, they
are false. Even though they are false, they can't not
sleep. If you don't sleep, you can't take it. Look at
Aniruddha who didn't sleep for a week and consequently went
blind! So, the Buddhas know all the different states of
mind of living beings. Each living being goes with its
kind. In the Ten Dharma Realms living beings hang out with
those in their own realm. Bodhisattvas do the deeds of Bodhisattvas. Arhats do Arhat's work. Gods do the deeds of
gods. People do people-type things. Asuras do asura things;
that is, they fight all day long. Hungry ghosts do hungry
ghost things, and animals do animal things. Hell-beings do
hellish things. Each follows its own kind.

The seventh is that they know where all paths lead.
If you cultivate the five precepts and ten good deeds, you
can be born in the heavens. If you cultivate the Dhyanas,
you can certify to the fruit. If you cultivate the six perfections and ten thousand conducts, you can become a Buddha.
If you create offenses, you can turn into a hungry ghost or
fall into hell. Whatever cause you plant, you reap that
fruit. If you plant a good cause, you reap a good fruit;
if you plant a bad cause, you reap a bad fruit.

There are ten powers, but they are inexhaustible, really. From ten you get a hundred, a thousand, ten thousand, a million, and so on.

AND HAVE PERFECTED THE THIRTY-TWO MARKS/ the thirty-two marks and eighty minor characteristics of a Buddha, THEN THAT IS GENUINE EXTINCTION/

Sutra: T. 27 b7

The Buddhas, the guiding masters,
Speak of Nirvana to give living beings rest,
But once they know that they are rested,
They lead them into the Buddhas' wisdom.

Outline:

> L2. Drawing the conclusion.

Commentary:

THE BUDDHAS, THE GUIDING MASTERS/ All the Buddhas are great leaders of living beings. SPEAK OF NIRVANA TO GIVE LIVING BEINGS A REST/They speak of Sound Hearer, Conditioned-Enlightened, and Bodhisattva Vehicles. They speak of Nirvana with residue. BUT ONCE THEY KNOW THAT THEY ARE RESTED/ Once they know living beings have rested up in the Transformation City, THEY LEAD THEM INTO THE BUDDHAS' WISDOM/ They lead living beings to become Buddhas and attain the Buddhas' wisdom.

The following verse is not in the Sutra text itself but is included as a praise and capsule summary.

Verse In Summary

    Moistening all the three dispositions
    The disciples receive the (Buddha's) kindness;
    But the transformed city is falsely created
        and is not real.
    One takes another look at the causes be-
        hind (the Buddha Great Penetrating)
        Wisdom Victory.)
    So the sixteen grandsons,
    In the eight directions, certify to a gold-
        en body.
    Homage to the Dharma Flower Assembly
        of Buddhas and Bodhisattvas.
    Homage to the Dharma Flower Assembly
        of Buddhas and Bodhisattvas.
    Homage to the Dharma Flower Assembly
        of Buddhas and Bodhisattvas.

(End of Chapter Seven, Roll Three, The
Wonderful Dharma Lotus Flower Sutra)

Index

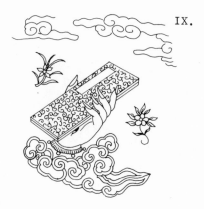

THE BUDDHIST TEXT TRANSLATION SOCIETY

Chairperson: The Venerable Tripitaka Master Hsüan Hua
Abbot of Gold Mountain Monastery and
Tathagata Monastery.
Chancellor of Dharma Realm Buddhist
University.
Professor of the Tripitaka and
the Dhyanas

PRIMARY TRANSLATING COMMITTEE:

Chairpersons: Bhikshuni Heng Yin
Bhikshuni Heng Ch'ih

Members: Bhikshu Heng Kuan
Bhikshu Heng K'ung
Bhikshu Heng Sure
Bhikshu Heng Shun
Bhikshu Heng Tso
Bhikshuni Heng Hsien
Bhikshuni Heng Ch'ing
Bhikshuni Heng Hua
Bhikshuni Heng Chen
Bhikshuni Heng Ming
Bhikshuni Heng Tao
Bhikshu Heng Teng
Bhikshu Heng Ch'i
Bhikshu Heng Kung

Upasaka Kuo Jung (R.B.) Epstein
Upasika Kuo Ts'an (Terri) Nicholson
Upasaka Kuo Chou (David) Rounds
Upasaka Chou Kuo Li
Professor Hsing Tsun Lee
Professor Wu-yi

REVIEWING COMMITTEE:

Chairpersons: Bhikshu Heng Tso
Upasaka Kuo Jung (R.B.) Epstein

Members: Bhikshu Heng Kuan
Bhikshu Heng Sure
Bhikshu Heng Teng
Bhikshu Heng Ch'i
Bhikshu Heng Kung
Bhikshuni Heng Yin
Bhikshuni Heng Ch'ih
Bhikshuni Heng Hsien
Bhikshuni Heng Ch'ing
Bhikshuni Heng Hua
Bhikshuni Heng Chen
Bhikshuni Heng Tao

Upasaka Kuo Jung (R.B.) Epstein
Upasika Hsieh Ping-ying
Upasika Kuo Ts'an Nicholson
Upasika Phuong Kuo Wu
Upasika Kuo Chin Vickers
Upasika Kuo Han Epstein
Upasaka Kuo Chou Rounds
Upasaka Chou Kuo Li
Professor Hsing Tsun Lee
Professor Wu-yi

EDITING COMMITTEE:

Chairperson: Bhikshu Heng Kuan

Members: Bhikshu Heng K'ung
Bhikshu Heng Sure
Bhikshu Heng Lai
Bhikshu Heng Shun
Bhikshu Heng Ch'au
Bhikshu Heng Ch'i
Bhikshuni Heng Yin
Bhikshuni Heng Ch'ih
Bhikshuni Heng Hsien
Bhikshuni Heng Ch'ing
Bhikshuni Heng Chu
Bhikshuni Heng Hua
Bhikshuni Heng Chen
Bhikshuni Heng Jieh
Bhikshuni Heng Ming
Bhikshuni Heng Tao

EDITING COMMITTEE, continued

Upasaka Kuo Jung (R.B.) Epstein
Upasaka Kuo Tsun (Randy) Dinwiddie
Upasika Kuo Shun Nolan
Upasika Kuo Chin (Janet) Vickers
Upasika Kuo Ts'an Nicholson
Upasaka Kuo Chou (David) Rounds
Upasika Kuo Lin (Nancy) Lethcoe
Upasaka Chou Kuo Li
Professor Hsing Tsun Lee
Professor Wu-yi
Professor Yu Kuo K'ung

CERTIFYING COMMITTEE:

Chairperson: *Venerable Tripitaka Master Hsüan Hua*

Members: Bhikshu Heng Kuan
Bhikshu Heng Sure
Bhikshu Heng Tso
Bhikshuni Heng Yin
Bhikshuni Heng Ch'ih
Bhikshuni Heng Hsien
Bhikshuni Heng Ch'ing
Bhikshuni Heng Tao

Upasaka Wong Kuo-chun
Upasaka Kuo Jung Epstein
Upasika T'an Kuo Shih
Upasika Kuo Chin Vickers

Transcribers: Bhikshuni
Heng-chai, Bhikshuni Heng-
wen, Upasika Kuo-li

BUDDHIST TEXT TRANSLATION SOCIETY
EIGHT REGULATIONS

A translator must free himself or herself from the motives of
personal fame and reputation.
A translator must cultivate an attitude free from arrogance
and conceit.
A translator must refrain from aggrandizing himself or herself
and denigrating others.
A translator must not establish himself or herself as the
standard of correctness and suppress the work of others with
his or her faultfinding.
A translator must take the Buddha-mind as his or her own mind.
A transaltor must use the wisdom of the Selective Dharma Eye
to determine true principles.
A translator must request the Elder Virtuous Ones of the ten
directions to certify his or her translations.
A translator must endeavor to propagate the teachings by
printing sutras, shastra texts, and vinaya texts when the
translations are certified as being correct.

PUBLICATIONS
OF THE
BUDDHIST TEXT
TRANSLATION SOCIETY

The Buddhist Text Translation Society is dedicated to making the genuine principles of the Buddhadharma available to the Western reader in a form that can be put directly into practice. Since 1972, the Society has been publishing English translations of Sutras (the sayings of the Buddha), instructional handbooks in meditation and moral conduct, biographies, poetry, and fiction. Each of the Society's Sutra translations is accompanied by a contemporary commentary spoken by the Venerable Master Hsuan Hua. The Venerable Master is the founder of Gold Mountain Monastery and the International Institute for the Translation of Buddhist Texts, in San Francisco, of the City of 10,000 Buddhas and Dharma Realm Buddist University in Mendocino County, California, and of Gold Wheel Temple in Los Angeles. The Venerable Master's sublime commentaries on the wonderful Dharma, given in daily public lectures, have been heard by sincere cultivators in America since 1962. For many years he has been working tirelessly to establish the proper Dharma in the West by providing clear explanations of the most important texts of the Buddhist Canon and by leading thousands of disciples-monks, nuns, laypeople, and students-along the Buddha's path to enlightenment through moral practice and spiritual discipline.

BUDDHIST SUTRAS:

The Dharma Flower (Lotus) Sutra, with commentary. *"Those of slight widsom who delight in lesser dharmas do not believe that they can become Buddhas. That is why we (the Buddhas) use expedient methods, discriminating and teaching the various stages. Although three vehicles are taught, it is only for the sake of instructing Bodhisattvas".* The Lotus Flower of the Wondrous Dharma Sutra is the king of all Buddhist Sutras because it is the final teaching of the Buddha in which he proclaimed the ultimate and only vehicle- the Buddha-vehicle. Vol. 1, Introduction, 85 pgs. $3.95, Vol. II, 324 pgs. $7.95, Vol. III, $7.95   Further volumes forthcoming.

The Flower Garland (Avatamsaka) Sutra:

Preface by T'ang Dynasty National Master Ch'ing Liang. *"Going and returning without any trace; Movement and stillness have one source. Embracing the multitude of wonders yet more remains; Transcending words and thought by far. This can only be the Dharmarealm!"* The succint verse commentary to the Avatamsaka Sutra by the Venerable T'ang Dynasty Master present the Sutra's principles in concise and elegant form, explained for modern readers in the appended commentary by the Ven. Master Hua. $9.00 Tentative Price.

The Ten Dwellings, Chapter Fifteen *with commentary. "All dharmas are apart from words and speech. Their nature is empty, still, extinct and uncreated. Desiring to understand this principle of reality, the Bodhisattva resolves to become enlightened."* The major stages passed through by Bodhisattvas after an initial perfection of the Ten Faiths are: the Ten Dwellings, the Ten Practices, the Ten Transferences, the Ten Grounds, Equal Enlightenment and Wonderful Enlightenment. During the course of the Ten Dwellings the Bodhisattva truly brings forth the great thought for Bodhi, is reborn in the household of the Thus Come One, and receives Annointment of the Crown. $6.95

The Ten Grounds, Chapter 26. *Part 1 with commentary. "As the traces of a bird as it wings its path though space are difficult to express, difficult to discern, so too are the principles of the Ten Grounds. From compassion, kindness, and the power of vows one can enter the practices of the Grounds and gradually the mind will become perfected."* Part One gives an explanation of the Bodhisattva's First Ground called 'happiness' in which the perfection of giving is brought to completion. $9.00 Tentative Price.

The Dharani Sutra, with commentary. *"World Honored One, I have a Great Compassion Dharanimantra which I now wish to speak so that all living beings might obtain peace and delight, be rid of every sickness, and attain long life; so that they might obtain prosperity, wipe away the evil karma of heavy offenses, seperate themselves from obstacles and hardships, grow in all the pure dharmas and in every kind of merit and virtue."* In the Dharani Sutra, the Bodhisattva Avalokiteshvara (Gwan Yin) shows how by the practice of compassion and the recitation of the Great Compassion Mantra we can rescue living beings in distress by means of wholesome magic and healing. Illustrated with woodcuts from the Secret School. 352 pgs., $12.00

The Sutra in Forty-two Sections, with commentary. *"When the Shramana who has left the home-life puts an end to his desires and drives away his longings, he knows the source of his own mind and penetrates to the profound principles of Buddhahood. He awakens to the Unconditioned, clinging to nothing within and seeking nothing without."* The Sutra in which the Buddha gives the essentials of the Path. 114 pgs. $4.00

The Sutra of the Past Vows of Earth Store Bodhisattva, with commentary. *"Earth Store Bodhisattva said, 'When the great ghost of impermanence arrives, the spirit roams in darkness and obscurity, not knowing what is offense and what is merit. For forty-nine days it is as if one were stunned and deaf, or as if in a court arguing karmic retribution. Once judgement has been fixed, rebirth is undergone in accordance with one's deeds.'"* One of the most popular Sutras in China, describing the heavens and hells, the workings of karma, and the virtue of filial piety. 235 pgs., $9.00 paper, $16.00 cloth.

The Sixth Patriarch's Sutra, with commentary. *"If you attend to others faults, your faultfinding itself is wrong. Others' faults I do not treat as wrong. My faults are my own transgressions. Simply cast out the mind that finds fault. Once cast away, troubles are gone. When hate and love don't block the mind, stretch out both legs and then lie down."* The classic Sutra on the life and teachings of the illiterate Patriarch, the Great Master Hui Neng. 380 pgs., $10.00 paper, $15.00 cloth.

The Shurangama Sutra, with commentary. *"The Buddha said, 'Hey, Ananda that is not your mind'. Startled, Ananda leapt from his seat, stood and put his palms together, and said to the Buddha, 'If this is not my mind, what is it?' The Buddha said to Ananda, 'It is your perception of false appearances based on external objects, which deludes your true nature and has caused you from beginningless time to your present life to recognize a thief as your son, to lose your eternal source, and to undergo the wheel's turning.'"* It is said, *"With the Shurangama one develops wisdom; with the Dharma Flower one becomes a Buddha."* Included in this Sutra is the Buddha's explanation of the 50 demonic states associated with the five skandhas. Vol. I 289 pgs., $8.50. vol. II $8.50 Further volumes forthcoming.

The Vajra Sutra, with commentary. *"All conditioned dharmas are like dreams, illusions, bubbles, shadows, like dew drops and a lightning flash; contemplate them thus."* Prajna or transcendental wisdom, the subject of this Sutra, is of central importance in the Buddha's teaching. The Buddha spent 20 years speaking the Prajna Sutras and declared that they would be disseminated to every land. 192 pgs. $8.00

The Amitabha Sutra, with commentary. *"Shariputra, if there is a good man or good woman who hears spoken 'Amitabha' and holds his name, whether for one day, two days, three, four, five days, six days, as long as seven days, with one heart unconfused, when this person approaches the end of life, before him will appear Amitabha and all the assembly of holy ones. When the end comes, his heart will be without inversion; in Amitabha's Land of Ultimate Bliss he will attain rebirth."* Shakyamuni Buddha spoke the Amitabha Sutra to let all living beings know of the power of Amitabha Buddha's great vows to lead all who recite his name with faith to rebirth in his Buddhaland the Land of Ultimate Bliss, where they may cultivate and quickly realize Buddhahood. 204 pgs., $8.00

The Heart Sutra and Verses Without a Stand, with commentary. *"Because nothing is attained, the Bodhisattva through reliance on prajna paramita is unimpeded in his mind. Because there is no impediment, he is not afraid and he leaves distorted dream-thinking far behind. Ultimately Nirvana."* The Heart Sutra exresses the essence of prajna paramita, the great and perfect wisdom taught by the Buddha. many practicing Buddhists recite the Sutra daily. The Venerable Master Hua's verses and commentary clearly explain each passage of the text, making this volume an excellent introduction to the basic concepts of the Buddhas's teaching. Bilingual edition, with English and Chinese on facing pages, $10.00 Tentative Price.

BUDDHIST PRACTICE:

The Shramanera Vinaya and Rules of Deportment, with commentary. *"Be kind and aid the needy, causing them to be at peace. If you see someone engaged in the act of killing, you should bring forth throughts of compassion."* The Buddha instructed his disciples to take the Vinaya (the moral code) for their teacher once he himself had entered Nirvana. Those who seek to end birth and death and to save all living beings must base their practice on proper morality. 112 pgs. $5.00

The Song of Enlightenment, with commentary. *"Only reach the root; have no concern for the branches. Like a pure crystal holding a precious moon. If this as-you-wish pearl can be understood, self and the benefit of others are forever unending."* The famous lyric poem of the state of the sage, by the Venerable Master Yung Chia of the T'ang Dynasty of China. Bilingual edition, with English translation and Chinese original on facing pages. $8.00, Tentative Price.

The Ten Dharma Realms Are Not Beyond A Single Thought. *"The way of men is harmony, with merit and error interspersed. On virtuous deeds you rise, offenses make you fall. It has nothing to do with anyone else at all."* A complete picture of Buddhist cosmology in verses; accompanied by an extensive commentary. 72 pgs. $4.00

Pure Land And Ch'an Dharma Talks. *"From limitless aeons past until the present we have accumulated uncountable states of mind in the field of our eighth consciousness. Sitting quietly allows these states to come forth in a way that they can be recognized, just like the moon's reflection in still water."* Instructions by the Venerable Master Hua in the practice of ch'an (Zen) meditation and reciting the Buddha's name. 72 pgs., $4.00

Buddha Root Farm. "Someone says, 'But the Western Land of Ultimate Bliss is so far away-hundreds of thousands of millions of Buddhalands-how can I go there? Can I take a plane? How much will the ticket cost? How much is the bus fare? Could I drive myself?' Don't worry about that. You can arrive in a single thought. You don't have to buy any tickets at all." Instructions by the Venerable Master Hua on the most widely used Buddhist meditation method: recitation of the name of the Buddha Amitabha of the Western Pure Land. 72 pgs. $4.00

Listen to Yourself. Think it Over. "Why should one sit in meditation? Sitting in meditation subdues the mind. When we sit we cause all the energy and blood in our body to return to its original source. If you apply your skill,...when the time comes...you will be the final victor." Instructions given by the Venerable Master Hua during a one-week Gwan Yin Bodhisattva Recitation and three-week Chan meditation session. $7.00, 153 pages.

Three Steps, One Bow. "Even before we left San Francisco to begin the pilgrimage, people were doubtful about how we would obtain the basic requirements for survival. But the Master had said that if one is completely sincere and genuine, survival would not be a problem. The Master has completely proved this in his own life, and after a while on our trip we too found it to be true without fail. We discovered very quickly, though, that what is tacitly assumed by this principle is equally true: if your heart is not sincere, survival will be a problem." Three Steps, One Bow is Heng Ju's and Heng Yo's own story of devotion, humor, and hardships overcome on their extraordinary 1,100 mile pilgrimage. In 1973 and 1974 with Heng Yo at his side, Bhikshu Heng Ju walked from San Francisco to Marblemount, Washington, bowing to the ground every third step, praying for peace for all humankind. 160 pgs. $5.95

With One Heart Bowing to the City of 10,000 Buddhas, "People we meet are not ashamed or afraid to admit they got on the wrong track and want to start again on the right foot. Open and energetic, a lot of folks are ready to 'return the light and look within.' But where to begin? '. . . where was there ever a person of wisdom, who got to see and hear the Buddha without cultivating pure vows and walking the same path the Buddha walked?' (FLOWER GARLAND SUTRA). The Master has stressed, 'Make Buddhism your personal responsibility.' This is what really counts: each person 'trying his best' to put down the false and find the true. What moves and inspires people is practice — 'pure vows and walking the road.' Talk is cheap." the moving daily record of two American monks' bowing pilgrimage (1977-1979) from Gold Wheel Temple in Los Angeles to the city of 10,000 Buddhas in Mendocino County in order to influence humankind to cease all hatred and hostility. Vol. I, 180 pgs. $6.00.

World Peace Gathering. A moving document of American Buddhism in action. Articles, poems, essays, and photos commemorating the successful completion of Bhikshu Heng Ju's and Bhikshu Heng Yo's pilgrimage in 1974. 128 pgs $5.00

BIOGRAPHICAL:

Records of the Life of the Venerable Master Hsuan Hua, Part I. "The Master was 19 years old when his mother passed away. At this time, he left the home life, taking the ten precepts of a Sramanera (novice monk). He then went to his mother's grave site, and built a 5' x 8' hut out of five-inch sorghum stalks. The hut kept out the wind and rain, but there was little difference between the inside and the outside. Here the Master observed the custom of filial piety by watching over his mother's grave for a period of three years. Clothed only in a rag robe, he endured the bitter Manchurian snow and the blazing summer sun. He ate only one meal a day and never slept lying down." An account of the Master's early years in China. 96 pgs. $5.00

Records of the Life of Chan Master Hsuan Hua, Part II. "The Master sat unmoving on the rock in the barren cave for several days and nights, only deciding to get up after about 100 hours of uninterrupted sitting. But when he tried to stand he found that his legs wouldn't move. Rather than giving in to an instinctive reaction of panic and concern for the welfare of his body the Master paid no attention to the paralysis, but simply continued to sit on the rock in the dank cave. He remained in the full lotus mediation posture day and night for two full weeks, and then gradually began to recover the use of his legs." The events of the Master's life as he cultivated and taught his followers in Hong Kong containing many photographs, poems, and stories. 229 pgs., $8.00.

FICTION:

Celebrisi's Journey A novel by David (Kuo Chou) Rounds. Where is the realm beyond the senses? What happens when a modern man sets out to find it? This is the story of a search pursued across the landscape of America from New Jersey to Maine to the Dakotas to California, through despair to understanding through the cloud of thoughts to the bright stillness, into the mind, beyond the self. 178 pgs. $4.00

Songs for Awakening, songs inspired by the teachings of Shakyamuni Buddha and the Venerable Master Hsuan Hua

VAJRA BODHI SEA

The monthly journal of the Sino American Buddhist Association since 1970, Vajra Bodhi Sea makes Buddhist writings and Buddhist news available to readers everywhere. Each issue contains Sutra translations, biographical sketches of high masters of antiquity, and biographies of contemporary Buddhist of the Sangha and lay communities. Also included are feature articles, world Buddhist news, poetry, book reviews, a series of Sanskrit lessons and vegetarian recipes. $22 for a one year subscription. $60 for a three year subscription. Beginning with the centennial issue (September 1978) Vajra Bodhi Sea has been published bilingually (Chinese and English)

A General Introduction To The Sino-American Buddhist Association. *A description of the aims, activities, and history of the Association, with poems, photos, and an emphasis on the Associations activities in San Francisco. 22 pgs. $2.00*

City of 10,000 Buddhas Color Brochure. *Over 30 color photos, of the new center for World Buddhism located in the fertile Ukiah Valley near Wonderful Enlightenment Mountain 100 miles north of San Francisco. Also includes many poems and brief descriptions of various activities of the City. 24 pgs. $2.00*

an affiliate of
The Sino-American Buddhist Association
1731 Fifteenth Street
San Francisco, California 94103
Telephone (415) 621-5202

Also from the Buddhist Text Translation Society:

Sutras:

AMITABHA SUTRA. This Sutra, which was spoken by the Buddha without
being formally requested, explains the causes of being reborn in
the Pure Land of Amitabha Buddha of limitless light. The commentary
contains extensive information on common Buddhist terms and
stories on all of the major Arhat disciples of the Buddha. 204 pps.,
$8.00. Also available in Spanish.

DHARANI SUTRA OF AVALOKITESHVARA BODHISATTVA. Tells the past
events in the lives of Avalokiteshvara and various ways of practicing the Great Compassion Mantra as well as the many benefits
gained from doing so. 210 pps., $6.00.

WONDERFUL DHARMA LOTUS FLOWER SUTRA (LOTUS SUTRA). Spoken in the
last period of the Buddha's teaching career, the Lotus proclaims the
ultimate principles of the Dharma which unites all teachings into
one vehicle. The following volumes have been published to date:
     Vol. I, Introduction. Discusses the Five Periods and Eight
Teachings of the T'ien-t'ai School and then analyzes the Five
Profound Meanings as they relate to the Sutra. Includes extensive
biography of Tripitaka Master Kumarajiva who translated the Sutra
from Sanskrit into Chinese. 85 pps., $3.95.
     Volume II, Chapter Two, Introduction. Describes the setting
for the speaking of the Sutra including the assembly who gathered
to hear it. Explains the meaning of the six portents and relates
the response of Maitreya Bodhisattva. 324 pps., $7.95.
     Vol. III, Expedient Devices. The Buddha emerges from samadhi
and speaks. After three requests, the Buddha again speaks and
proclaims for the first time the doctrine of universal salvation,
unique to the Lotus teaching.
     Volume IV., Chapter III, A Parable. The Buddha explains the
nature of his teaching by means of the analogy of an elder who tries
to rescue his five hundred children who are absorbed in their play
in the burning house. 371 pps., $8.95.
     Vol. V. Belief and Understanding, Chapter Four. Four of the
Buddha's foremost Arhat disciples tell a story about a child who
ran away from home and many years later returned to his father,
to express their happines upon hearing that they, too, could become Buddhas in the future. 200 pps. $6.95.
     Vol. VI. Medicinal Herbs, Chapter Five, and Conferring
Predictions, Chapter Six. 161 pps., $6.95. The Buddha uses the
analogy of a rain-cloud to illustrate how his teaching benefits
all beings with total impartiality and gives specific predictions
for the future attainment of Buddhahood for the four great Arhats.
616 pps., $6.95

FLOWER ADORNMENT SUTRA VERSE PREFACE, by National Master Ch'ing-liang. A succinct verse commentary by T'ang Dynasty National Master Ch'ing-liang. Gives a complete overview of all fundamental principles contained in the Sutra. First English translation. Bi-lingual edition. 224 pps., $7.00.

HEART SUTRA AND VERSES WITHOUT A STAND. Probably the most popular Sutra in the world today, it is recited daily in most monasteries. The tesxt explains the meaning of Prajna-paramita, the perfection of wisdom, which is able to clearly perceive the emptiness of all dharmas. Each line is accompanied by an eloquent verse by the Venerabla Master Hua, as well as commentary containing explanation of all fundamental concepts. Available Soon.

SHURANGAMA SUTRA. Gives the most detailed explanation of the Buddha's psychology. Includes an analysis of the mind. Twenty-five enlightened sages tell how they became enlightened. The following volumes are available now:
    Vol. I, The Venerable Ananda presents seven ideas on the location of the mind, and the Buddha shows how each one is in-correct. He then explains the roots of the false and the true. 289 pps., $8.50.
    Vol.II, The Buddha explains individual and collective karma, and reveals the true mind by showing ten different aspects of the seeing-nature. 212 pps., $8.50.
    Vol. III. The Buddha gives a clear description of internal and external elemental forces of the universe. 240 pps., $8.50.

SIXTH PATRIARCH'S SUTRA. One of the foremost scriptures of Ch'an Buddhism, this Sutra describes the life and teachings of the illiterate Patriarch Great Master Hui-neng. 235 pps., $10.00. Also in hardcover, $15.00.

SUTRA IN 42 SECTIONS. In this Sutra, the first to be transported and translated in China from India, the Buddha gives the most fundamental and practice instructions in practicing the Dharma, emphasizing the cardinal virtues of renunciation, contentment, and patience. 114 pps., $4.00.

SUTRA OF THE PAST VOWS OF EARTH STORE BODHISATTVA. This Sutra tells how Earth Store Bodhisattva attained his position as one of the greatest Bodhisattvas, foremost in vows, and also the workings of karma, how being undergo rebirth,and various kinds of retribution. First translation into English. 235 pps. $9.00. Hardcover $16.00.

VAJRA-PRAJNA-PARAMITA SUTRA. One of the most popular scriptures, the Sutra explains the nature of the perfection of wisdom and how the Buddha relies on it to teach and transform many beings throughout many lives. 192 pps. $8.00.

BIOGRAPHY:

RECORDS OF THE LIFE OF THE VENERABLE MASTER HSUAN-HUA. The life
and teachings of the Venerale Master from his birthplace, China,
to the present time in America by his followers. Two volumes. Vol. I,
96. pps., $5.00. (Also in Spanish). Vol. II, 229 pps., $8.00/

WORLD PEACE GATHERING. A collection of instructional talks on
Buddhism commemorating the successful completion of the bowing
pilgrimage of Bhikshus Heng-ju and Heng-yo. 128 pps., $5.00.

WITH ONE HEART BOWING TO THE CITY OF 10,000 Buddhas. The journal
of American Bhikshus Heng-sure and Heng-chau, who made a "three
steps, one bow" pilgrimage from Gold Wheel Temple in Los Angeles
to the City of Ten Thousand Buddhas (110 miles north of San Francisco. Vol. I., 180 pps. $6.00. Vol. II., 322 pps., $7.50, Vol.
III., 154 pps., $6.00.

FICTION:

CELEBRESI'S JOURNEY. A novel by David Rounds describing the
events in a modern American's quest for enlightenment. 178 pps.,
$4.00.

MUSIC:

SONGS FOR AWAKENING. Words and music of over forty modern
American Buddhist songs, indexed according to title and first
line, with drawing, woodcuts, and photographs. A fine gift to
intorduce people to Buddhism. 112 pps. $7.95.

AWAKENING. 12" Stereo LP, record album of Buddhist songs in
western style. Interprets the Buddha's teaching in distinctly
western musical styles ranging from pop to rock to folk, making
this album and true trans-cultural fusion. $8.00 includes postage
and handling.